Quality Management in the Digital Age

Digital Quality Management in the Age of Transformation

Table of Content

Preface

In today's fast-paced, technology-driven world, quality management is undergoing a profound transformation. Organizations across industries are moving beyond traditional practices, embracing digital tools, and harnessing data in unprecedented ways to meet evolving standards and customer expectations. This book, Digital Quality Management in the Age of Transformation, is a guide for navigating the dynamic intersection of quality and technology, providing insights into the tools, techniques, and strategies essential for a modern approach to quality assurance and control.

The journey of digital transformation in quality management requires a comprehensive understanding of emerging technologies like artificial intelligence (AI), the Internet of Things (IoT), and blockchain. These tools hold tremendous potential to improve accuracy, accelerate response times, and enhance traceability. Yet, with opportunities come challenges: leaders and quality teams must adapt to new ways of working, address skill gaps, and ensure data privacy and cybersecurity. Each chapter in this book has been crafted to address these critical issues, providing readers with a practical foundation to implement and manage digital quality initiatives.

This book also emphasizes the importance of a customer-centric approach in the digital era. As customer expectations continue to grow, quality management must extend beyond meeting specifications, focusing on customer satisfaction, real-time feedback, and collaborative partnerships with suppliers and stakeholders. To that end, we explore how digital tools can support responsive, data-driven decision-making and foster an organizational culture committed to quality and continuous improvement.

In Digital Quality Management in the Age of Transformation, readers will find a holistic view of modern quality management, from building data-driven quality cultures to applying agile methodologies, ensuring compliance, and managing risks in digital environments. Each section combines theory with practical insights, industry examples, and case studies that showcase how leading organizations have successfully implemented digital quality practices.

Whether you are a quality manager, executive, or professional at any level of experience, this book offers you the knowledge and tools to lead in an era where quality is both a strategic advantage and an evolving challenge. As you read, I hope you gain not only a better understanding of digital quality management but also the inspiration to innovate, adapt, and make quality a driving force in your organization's success.

Welcome to the journey of digital transformation in quality management. May it empower you to achieve excellence in every product, process, and customer experience you deliver.

Chapter 1: Introduction to Quality Management in the Digital Age

1.1 Historical Overview of Quality Management

Quality management has been central to organizational success for centuries. Originally focused on inspection, it evolved over the 20th century to embrace broader strategies, such as Quality Assurance (QA) and Total Quality Management (TQM). These methodologies were pioneered by figures who revolutionized the way organizations approach quality, and their work laid the foundation for today's practices.

Evolution from Quality Inspection to Quality Assurance and TQM

In its earliest forms, quality management was a straightforward inspection process designed to identify and remove defective products. During the Industrial Revolution, large-scale manufacturing increased demand for a systematic approach to ensuring quality, giving rise to quality inspection as a formal practice. However, as production volumes and complexities grew, it became evident that simply detecting defects was insufficient. Quality issues needed to be addressed earlier in the process.

By the mid-20th century, Quality Assurance became more widely implemented. Rather than merely identifying defects at the end, QA focuses on preventing defects throughout the production process. This shift represented a proactive approach where quality checks are embedded in each step, from raw material selection to final output.

TQM emerged as a comprehensive philosophy by the 1980s. It extends beyond product inspection and production process controls to involve every function and employee in an organization. TQM promotes a culture of continuous improvement, where quality is viewed as a shared responsibility. The framework focuses on meeting customer expectations, emphasizing customer satisfaction as the measure of quality. This philosophy has influenced various methodologies like Six Sigma, Lean, and Kaizen, each of which seeks to achieve operational excellence by reducing waste and improving processes.

Pioneers in Quality Management

Three influential figures—W. Edwards Deming, Joseph M. Juran, and Genichi Taguchi—played critical roles in developing modern quality management concepts. Their contributions helped shape the quality discipline into a systematic science focused on efficiency and continuous improvement.

W. Edwards Deming

Deming's work in post-war Japan introduced statistical quality control, emphasizing that quality is not solely a product of final inspection but rather a result of robust processes. His Deming Cycle (Plan-Do-Check-Act) became a fundamental model for continuous improvement. Deming advocated for a holistic approach to quality, where every member of an organization contributes to the process.

Joseph M. Juran

Known for the Juran Trilogy, which focuses on quality planning, quality control, and quality improvement, Juran emphasized that quality must be managed rather than controlled. He advocated for a top-down approach, where leaders create an environment that supports quality at all levels. His emphasis on quality leadership has left a lasting impact on organizations' approach to continuous improvement.

Genichi Taguchi

Taguchi's contributions lie in his approach to designing quality into products from the beginning. He developed the Taguchi Method, which includes robust design and experimentation to reduce variability and optimize performance. His insights are especially relevant today in an era where customer expectations for consistent quality are high.

1.2 The Impact of Digital Transformation on Quality Management

The arrival of digital technologies has profoundly altered the landscape of quality management. Tools such as data analytics, artificial intelligence (AI), Internet of Things (IoT), and blockchain have introduced new methods for improving, monitoring, and ensuring quality throughout the production process. As organizations move towards digitalization, the potential for predictive and proactive quality management has increased, enabling a new era of continuous improvement.

Digitalization in the Quality Domain

Digital transformation introduces both challenges and opportunities in quality management. Traditionally, quality management involved sampling, manual inspections, and process monitoring, all of which are limited by human capacity and variability. Digital tools, however, can enhance these activities by providing deeper insights, faster detection of issues, and more comprehensive quality data.

For instance, the use of IoT in manufacturing allows for real-time monitoring of equipment and production parameters. With sensors embedded in machines, data on temperature, pressure, and other critical factors are constantly transmitted, enabling immediate interventions when thresholds are crossed. This capability allows companies to prevent defects before they occur, enhancing quality assurance processes.

Data analytics and AI facilitate predictive quality management, which is essential in identifying trends, forecasting potential issues, and preemptively addressing them. By analyzing large volumes of historical and real-time data, AI algorithms can recognize patterns that indicate a high probability of defects, enabling proactive quality management strategies.

Importance of Adapting to Digital Innovations for Continuous Quality Improvement

Continuous quality improvement has long been an objective of quality management, but digitalization accelerates this process. Organizations that adapt to digital innovations can achieve higher levels of quality more efficiently. Traditional continuous improvement methods, such as the Deming Cycle, are enhanced by digital tools, allowing organizations to iterate and adjust processes more rapidly than ever.

Digital transformation also makes it possible to implement more advanced quality metrics and KPIs, making it easier to measure aspects of quality that were once difficult to assess. For example, digital systems can provide real-time visibility into defect rates, customer satisfaction, and production efficiency, enabling companies to act on this data immediately rather than waiting for periodic reports. These technologies support the Voice of the Customer (VoC) initiatives by collecting customer feedback through digital channels, translating customer expectations into actionable data, and improving products or services accordingly.

Digital transformation also introduces challenges that organizations must address. The adaptation of quality processes to digital tools requires training, new skill sets, and overcoming resistance to change. Furthermore, organizations must invest in cybersecurity and data governance to protect the integrity and confidentiality of their digital quality data.

1.3 Purpose and Scope of the Book

This book explores the intersection of traditional quality management principles and modern digital tools, offering insights and guidance on how quality management can thrive in the digital age. It provides readers with a roadmap to adapt their quality management practices to a world of rapid technological advancement, focusing on the practical applications and challenges that come with digital transformation.

Overview of Key Themes

Foundations of Quality Management

Before diving into digital advancements, understanding the basic principles of quality management is essential. This book revisits these principles, showing how they continue to apply even in a digital context. Concepts such as TQM, Lean, and Six Sigma remain relevant, but digital tools offer new ways to implement these methodologies effectively.

Digital Transformation in Quality

The digital age introduces various technologies—AI, IoT, Big Data, and blockchain—that have the potential to revolutionize quality management. This book examines each of these technologies, discussing their applications in quality improvement, monitoring, and control. By understanding these tools, organizations can make better-informed decisions on how to integrate them into their quality processes.

Data-Driven Quality Decisions

The rise of digital data provides an unprecedented opportunity for making data-driven decisions. This book explores the importance of data quality, analytics, and predictive models in decision-making, helping organizations leverage data to improve quality outcomes and customer satisfaction.

Agile and Customer-Centric Quality Management

As organizations adopt digital tools, they also need to adapt their processes to meet rapidly evolving customer expectations. This book highlights agile methodologies and customer-centric approaches that enhance responsiveness, enabling organizations to quickly address quality concerns and improve customer experiences.

Building a Digital-First Quality Culture

Adapting to the digital age requires more than just implementing new tools; it demands a cultural shift. The book delves into how organizations can foster a quality-centric mindset within their teams, where employees at all levels contribute to quality improvements through digital means.

Importance of Digital Quality Management

With digital transformation reshaping industries, quality management must also evolve to remain effective. Quality is no longer just a measure of product performance but a measure of how well an organization meets customer expectations and adapts to changes. By integrating digital tools, organizations can achieve faster and more reliable results, reduce human error, and make better-informed decisions.

Chapter 2: Foundations of Quality Management Principles

Quality management is a cornerstone of organizational success across industries. It is a discipline that involves planning, controlling, and improving quality across all functions within an organization. This chapter will cover the fundamental principles that provide the basis for quality management. We will explore the key concepts of Quality Assurance (QA) and Quality Control (QC), as well as core principles like customer focus, continuous improvement, and evidence-based decision-making, which guide the practices within quality management systems.

2.1 Core Quality Management Concepts

Quality management encompasses various practices, methodologies, and tools designed to ensure that products, services, and processes consistently meet or exceed customer expectations. The distinction between Quality Assurance and Quality Control is foundational to understanding quality management. Beyond these concepts, quality management is also defined by a set of guiding principles that shape its practices across industries.

Definitions: Quality Assurance vs. Quality Control

The terms "Quality Assurance" and "Quality Control" are sometimes used interchangeably, but they represent distinct functions within quality management. Both aim to improve quality, yet they achieve this goal in different ways and at different stages in the production or service lifecycle.

Quality Assurance (QA)

Quality Assurance is a proactive, process-oriented approach to managing quality. QA involves setting up systems, procedures, and practices that will prevent defects and ensure consistent performance.

It emphasizes planning, systematic processes, and ongoing monitoring to maintain quality throughout production or service delivery. The primary goal of QA is to prevent errors by creating a structured process that adheres to standards and best practices.

QA activities include:

Defining quality standards and establishing requirements.

Developing quality processes and control points.

Conducting regular audits and process assessments.

Providing training to ensure employees follow quality guidelines.

By implementing QA practices, organizations aim to build quality into their products and services from the beginning. For example, an automobile manufacturer might use QA practices to standardize design specifications, ensuring that each part aligns with safety and quality standards before production begins.

Quality Control (QC)

Quality Control, on the other hand, is a reactive, product-oriented approach focused on detecting defects. QC involves inspecting and testing products or services to identify deviations from quality standards. Unlike QA, which focuses on preventing defects, QC focuses on identifying and correcting them after they occur. QC practices are typically applied during and after production to ensure that products meet the established quality standards.

QC activities include:

Conducting product inspections at various stages of production.

Testing samples from production batches.

Analyzing data to identify trends in product quality.

Implementing corrective actions when defects are found.

QC is essential in detecting issues that may have escaped the preventative processes of QA. For instance, a pharmaceutical company might perform batch testing to ensure that each drug meets potency requirements before it is released for distribution.

In summary, while Quality Assurance is about establishing a quality system to prevent issues, Quality Control is about testing and inspection to catch issues that may arise. Together, they form a complete approach to quality management, with QA focusing on processes and QC on product or service outcomes.

Key Principles of Quality Management

In addition to the distinction between QA and QC, quality management is guided by core principles that have been established through research, industry standards, and best practices. These principles provide a framework for organizations to build robust quality systems, improve customer satisfaction, and achieve sustainable success.

Customer Focus

Customer focus is the foundational principle of quality management and lies at the heart of every successful quality initiative. This principle asserts that an organization's primary goal should be to meet or exceed customer expectations. Customers are the ultimate judges of quality, and their satisfaction is the most important measure of a product or service's success.

Understanding Customer Needs

To focus on customers, organizations must first understand their needs, preferences, and expectations. This requires gathering feedback, conducting surveys, and analyzing customer data to gain insights into what customers value most. For instance, a technology company might conduct regular user research to identify pain points in their software and prioritize features that enhance the user experience.

Delivering Value

Customer focus involves not only understanding what customers want but also delivering value through high-quality products and services. It means ensuring that every aspect of production, from raw materials to delivery, aligns with customer needs. This approach encourages businesses to prioritize quality in every step of the process, resulting in improved customer satisfaction, loyalty, and repeat business.

Building Long-Term Relationships

Organizations that prioritize customer focus tend to build stronger, long-term relationships with their clients. By consistently meeting or exceeding expectations, they foster trust and loyalty. Customer focus thus promotes a culture of continuous improvement, as organizations strive to maintain high standards and adapt to changing customer needs.

Measuring Customer Satisfaction

Customer satisfaction is a key metric in quality management. By regularly measuring satisfaction levels, organizations can assess their performance and identify areas for improvement. This data-driven approach enables them to make adjustments based on real feedback rather than assumptions, aligning their quality efforts with customer expectations.

In quality-focused organizations, every employee and function, from R&D to after-sales support, contributes to enhancing customer satisfaction. This commitment to customer-centric quality is crucial for an organization's growth and competitiveness in the market.

Continuous Improvement

Continuous improvement, or Kaizen in Japanese, is a core quality principle that emphasizes the need for constant progress in every process, product, and service. This principle ensures that organizations remain agile, innovative, and able to respond to changes in customer expectations and market conditions. Continuous improvement is central to methodologies like Lean, Six Sigma, and TQM, which aim to eliminate waste, reduce variability, and enhance efficiency.

Setting Incremental Goals

Continuous improvement involves setting small, achievable goals rather than attempting drastic changes. This approach makes improvements manageable and fosters a culture of regular progress. For instance, a manufacturer may set incremental goals for reducing waste by 5% each quarter rather than a sweeping reduction target. Such incremental goals create a steady momentum for improvement.

Encouraging Employee Involvement

Employees at all levels contribute to continuous improvement. When employees are encouraged to suggest improvements and identify inefficiencies, they become active participants in quality management. Engaging employees also enhances job satisfaction and creates a culture of shared responsibility for quality. Many organizations implement suggestion systems or quality circles where teams regularly meet to discuss potential improvements.

Using Quality Tools for Improvement

Continuous improvement is supported by various quality tools and techniques, including root cause analysis, the PDCA (Plan-Do-Check-Act) cycle, and Six Sigma methodologies. These tools help organizations systematically address issues and develop solutions based on data rather than assumptions. For instance, the PDCA cycle enables organizations to test small changes, assess their impact, and make necessary adjustments for ongoing improvement.

Monitoring and Analyzing Performance

Measuring performance is essential to identify areas for improvement. Organizations must establish quality metrics that track efficiency, defect rates, customer complaints, and other indicators. Continuous improvement involves using these metrics to pinpoint bottlenecks, inefficiencies, or areas where quality standards are not met. Data-driven insights enable targeted improvements and more efficient processes.

Evidence-Based Decision-Making

Evidence-based decision-making is the principle of using data, facts, and research to guide quality management decisions. This approach contrasts with decision-making based on intuition or assumptions, ensuring that changes and improvements are driven by objective data and analyses. Evidence-based decision-making is central to modern quality management, where technology and data analytics provide unprecedented insight into processes, customer behavior, and product performance.

Gathering Accurate Data

The foundation of evidence-based decision-making is accurate and reliable data. Quality management systems often rely on data from production processes, customer feedback, and market research. By collecting data at every stage of production, organizations can track product quality in real time and make informed decisions based on the latest information.

Analyzing Data with Statistical Tools

Statistical analysis is a powerful tool in quality management, enabling organizations to identify trends, patterns, and root causes of issues. Techniques like statistical process control (SPC), control charts, and hypothesis testing allow quality managers to detect deviations, measure process performance, and make objective decisions. For example, control charts help monitor production consistency, enabling timely intervention if data points fall outside established control limits.

Predictive and Preventive Quality Measures

Evidence-based decision-making is critical for predictive and preventive quality measures, which use historical data to anticipate issues before they arise. By leveraging predictive analytics, organizations can identify risk factors for defects and address them proactively. Preventive measures reduce costs associated with defects, recalls, and customer dissatisfaction, ultimately contributing to a more robust quality management system.

Benchmarking and Continuous Monitoring

Evidence-based decisions require benchmarking performance against industry standards and internal targets. Organizations must continuously monitor their quality metrics to assess performance and identify opportunities for improvement. Regular monitoring helps them maintain high standards and adapt to changes in demand, technology, and competition.

Documentation and Knowledge Sharing

Evidence-based decision-making encourages organizations to document findings and best practices. This knowledge-sharing culture ensures that valuable insights are retained and can be applied to future decisions. Documentation not only supports consistency in quality but also provides a reference for training and continuous improvement initiatives.

In summary, evidence-based decision-making is a disciplined approach that reduces risk and enhances quality by ensuring decisions are based on objective data. This principle empowers organizations to move away from reactive problem-solving towards proactive quality management.

These foundational principles—customer focus, continuous improvement, and evidence-based decision-making—form the core of effective quality management systems. When organizations embrace these principles, they create a culture that prioritizes excellence, fosters innovation, and maintains a competitive edge.

2.2 Traditional Tools and Methods

Here is an in-depth look at the traditional tools and methods that have shaped quality management practices over time, including frameworks like Six Sigma, Lean, Kaizen, and Total Quality Management (TQM), as well as traditional quality tools such as control charts, Pareto analysis, and Fishbone diagrams.

2.2 Traditional Tools and Methods in Quality Management

For decades, organizations across industries have relied on structured methodologies and tools to improve quality, reduce waste, and optimize processes. Traditional frameworks such as Six Sigma, Lean, Kaizen, and Total Quality Management (TQM) offer systematic approaches for achieving operational excellence and continuous improvement. Within these methodologies, quality professionals use a variety of tools, including control charts, Pareto analysis, and Fishbone diagrams, to identify and eliminate inefficiencies and enhance product or service quality. This section provides an overview of these established methodologies and tools, which continue to play an essential role in quality management.

Overview of Six Sigma, Lean, Kaizen, and TQM

Each of these methodologies has a unique focus, approach, and set of principles, but they all share a common goal: to enhance quality and efficiency. Understanding the differences and applications of each approach can help organizations select the most appropriate framework for their specific quality goals.

Six Sigma

Six Sigma is a data-driven methodology that aims to improve process performance by reducing variability and eliminating defects. Developed by Motorola in the 1980s, Six Sigma uses statistical methods to achieve near-perfect quality levels, with a target of only 3.4 defects per million opportunities.

Core Concepts of Six Sigma

The Six Sigma approach is built on two core methodologies:

DMAIC (Define, Measure, Analyze, Improve, Control): Used for improving existing processes by systematically identifying and addressing root causes of defects.

DMADV (Define, Measure, Analyze, Design, Verify): Applied for designing new processes or products to ensure they meet customer requirements from the outset.

Role of Statistical Analysis

Six Sigma places a heavy emphasis on statistical analysis to identify variations and measure process capability. By using tools like control charts, histograms, and process capability indices, Six Sigma practitioners can make data-driven decisions to improve quality.

Certification Levels

Six Sigma includes a structured certification hierarchy, commonly represented by belt levels (Yellow, Green, Black, and Master Black Belt), each indicating a practitioner's level of expertise. Organizations often invest in Six Sigma training to ensure that quality improvement efforts are led by skilled professionals.

By focusing on reducing defects and variations, Six Sigma helps organizations achieve greater consistency and reliability in their products and services.

Lean

Lean is a methodology centered on maximizing customer value by minimizing waste. Originally derived from the Toyota Production System, Lean aims to streamline processes, reduce lead times, and improve quality by eliminating activities that do not add value.

Core Principles of Lean

Lean operates on five core principles:

Identify Value: Understand what customers value and focus resources on those activities.

Map the Value Stream: Analyze the process steps to identify and eliminate waste.

Create Flow: Ensure that the production flow is smooth and efficient, with minimal disruptions.

Establish Pull: Use a demand-based system to produce only what is needed, reducing excess inventory.

Pursue Perfection: Engage in continuous improvement to refine processes and eliminate all forms of waste.

Types of Waste

Lean defines seven types of waste, known as "Muda," which include overproduction, waiting, transport, extra processing, inventory, motion, and defects. Lean practitioners use tools like value stream mapping, 5S, and Kanban to identify and reduce these wastes.

Continuous Improvement Culture

Lean promotes a culture of continuous improvement and employee involvement. By encouraging employees to identify inefficiencies and suggest improvements, Lean organizations create a sustainable approach to quality and operational excellence.

Kaizen

Kaizen, a Japanese term meaning "change for the better," is both a philosophy and a methodology for continuous improvement. Unlike other quality management methodologies that may focus on large-scale improvements, Kaizen emphasizes small, incremental changes that add up to significant long-term results.

Core Philosophy of Kaizen

The Kaizen philosophy is built on the belief that everyone, from top management to frontline workers, can contribute to improvements. Kaizen encourages employees to continuously look for ways to improve their tasks and processes, regardless of their position or expertise.

Kaizen Events

Kaizen events, also known as "blitzes," are short, focused improvement sessions where cross-functional teams work on solving specific issues. These events usually last a few days and aim to generate quick wins and actionable improvements that can be implemented immediately.

Principles of Kaizen

The key principles of Kaizen include teamwork, personal discipline, quality circles, and a focus on continuous learning. Organizations that adopt Kaizen typically create a workplace culture that values and rewards proactive problem-solving and collaboration.

Kaizen is particularly effective in creating a culture of sustained improvement, as it empowers employees to take ownership of quality at every level.

Total Quality Management (TQM)

Total Quality Management (TQM) is an organizational approach that emphasizes the need for quality in every aspect of operations. It is a comprehensive management philosophy that integrates quality into every organizational process, aiming to achieve long-term customer satisfaction and operational excellence.

Core Elements of TQM

TQM is based on the following elements:

Customer Focus: Understanding and meeting customer needs.

Leadership: Commitment from top management to drive quality initiatives.

Employee Involvement: Engaging employees at all levels in quality efforts.

Process Approach: Focusing on improving processes rather than individual performance.

System Integration: Ensuring that all departments and functions work cohesively towards quality objectives.

Continuous Improvement: Consistently working towards enhancing processes, products, and services.

Quality Circles

A key feature of TQM is the use of quality circles—small groups of employees who meet regularly to discuss quality issues and develop solutions. This encourages a collaborative approach to quality, fostering a sense of responsibility and teamwork across departments.

Long-Term Orientation

TQM focuses on building a sustainable quality system that delivers long-term benefits, such as higher customer satisfaction, improved employee morale, and competitive advantage.

Traditional Quality Tools

Within these quality management frameworks, several tools have become essential for analyzing, controlling, and improving quality. These tools are often referred to as the "Seven Basic Quality Tools" and are widely used across industries.

Control Charts

Control charts are used to monitor process performance over time and detect variations that may indicate issues. These charts plot data points against a set of control limits, helping quality practitioners distinguish between normal variation (common cause) and unusual variation (special cause).

Application

Control charts are commonly used in Six Sigma and Lean projects to ensure that processes remain stable and predictable. By analyzing trends and patterns in control charts, practitioners can identify when a process goes out of control and needs corrective action.

Types of Control Charts

There are various types of control charts, including:

X-bar and R Chart: Monitors the process mean and range for continuous data.

P Chart: Tracks the proportion of defective items in a sample.

C Chart: Monitors the number of defects per unit for attribute data.

Pareto Analysis

Pareto analysis, based on the 80/20 rule, is a decision-making tool that helps prioritize issues by identifying the most significant contributors to a problem. It suggests that 80% of problems are often caused by 20% of the factors, allowing organizations to focus their resources on the most impactful issues.

Application

Pareto analysis is widely used to identify root causes of defects, customer complaints, and other quality issues. For example, a manufacturing company may use Pareto analysis to determine which types of defects are responsible for most of its quality issues, thereby focusing on the biggest sources of problems.

Pareto Chart

A Pareto chart is a visual representation of Pareto analysis, typically displaying categories of issues along the x-axis and their frequency or impact along the y-axis. This helps quality managers quickly identify which categories contribute the most to a particular problem.

Fishbone Diagrams

Fishbone diagrams, also known as cause-and-effect or Ishikawa diagrams, help identify potential causes of a problem by categorizing factors that contribute to an effect. This tool is useful for root cause analysis and is often used during brainstorming sessions to organize ideas and identify the main contributors to quality issues.

Structure

The fishbone diagram resembles a fish skeleton, with the "head" representing the problem and "bones" branching out to show possible causes. Categories often include "People," "Process," "Material," "Equipment," "Environment," and "Methods."

Application

Fishbone diagrams are frequently used in conjunction with other tools, such as control charts and Pareto analysis, to drill down into the root causes of issues. By visually mapping out causes, teams can systematically address each factor and work towards a solution.

These traditional tools and methods provide a strong foundation for quality management. By implementing methodologies like Six Sigma, Lean, Kaizen, and TQM, and by utilizing tools such as control charts, Pareto analysis, and Fishbone diagrams, organizations can build robust quality systems that lead to improved performance, reduced waste, and increased customer satisfaction.

2.3 Challenges in Traditional Quality Management

As organizations navigate a rapidly changing digital landscape, traditional quality management approaches face numerous challenges that affect their effectiveness. While methodologies like Six Sigma, Lean, Kaizen, and Total Quality Management (TQM) have been essential to improving quality and reducing waste, their conventional frameworks and tools have limitations when applied to the fast-paced, data-driven world of digital transformation. This section will explore these challenges, emphasizing how digitalization is reshaping quality expectations and demanding a shift from traditional quality methods.

Limitations of Conventional Quality Approaches

Traditional quality management methodologies were developed for production environments where processes were stable, and changes occurred relatively gradually. However, in the context of modern business, where technological advances drive frequent shifts, these methods may struggle to keep up. Here are some core limitations of traditional quality management approaches in today's digital age:

1. Rigidity and Inflexibility in Rapidly Changing Environments

Traditional quality management methodologies, such as Six Sigma and TQM, rely on structured, step-by-step processes to identify and address quality issues. However, this rigidity can be a drawback in the digital age, where speed and adaptability are paramount. For example:

Six Sigma emphasizes a data-driven, disciplined approach with multiple steps (e.g., DMAIC: Define, Measure, Analyze, Improve, Control) that may be time-consuming to implement, especially in fast-paced industries.

Lean methodologies focus on incremental improvements and waste reduction, which, while effective, may not be agile enough to meet rapid, often unpredictable shifts in customer expectations and market demands.

In today's digital world, companies must continuously evolve their processes, products, and services to stay competitive. Traditional methods often require lengthy analysis and planning phases, which can slow down decision-making, making it challenging for organizations to respond quickly to market changes.

2. Limited Ability to Handle Large Volumes of Data

Modern quality management increasingly depends on data analytics, machine learning, and artificial intelligence (AI) to generate insights and drive decision-making. Traditional quality tools, however, are often limited to manual data analysis and visualization methods, which can be time-consuming and inadequate for handling large volumes of real-time data.

Control Charts, Pareto Analysis, and Fishbone Diagrams are effective for examining historical data and identifying patterns, but they fall short when it comes to processing and analyzing vast amounts of data from multiple sources in real-time.

Conventional quality methods may not fully utilize data from advanced sources, such as IoT sensors, cloud-based platforms, and big data analytics, limiting their ability to predict issues, identify trends, or make proactive improvements.

With the rise of big data, traditional quality management lacks the tools to integrate, analyze, and leverage data to drive predictive insights and optimization on a large scale. The inability to process high volumes of data effectively creates a bottleneck in decision-making and undermines the responsiveness of traditional quality management.

3. Inadequate Real-Time Monitoring and Response

Digital transformation has heightened the importance of real-time monitoring and swift response to quality issues. While traditional quality management focuses on statistical process control and periodic checks, these methods are not always conducive to instant feedback and continuous monitoring.

Lean and Six Sigma methodologies often require a series of sequential steps to identify, analyze, and resolve issues. In rapidly changing digital environments, however, by the time an issue is identified and resolved using these traditional approaches, it may already be outdated or have impacted the customer experience.

Real-time quality monitoring, now possible with IoT devices and AI-based systems, offers continuous quality assessment. However, traditional quality management methods lack the ability to take advantage of these technologies, resulting in a delayed response to quality deviations and potential customer dissatisfaction.

This gap is critical in industries like e-commerce, telecommunications, and software development, where quality issues must be addressed instantaneously to prevent service disruptions, product defects, or negative customer experiences.

4. Limited Scalability for Complex, Global Operations

As companies expand globally and supply chains become increasingly complex, traditional quality management approaches can face scalability challenges. Each quality management system (QMS) must address various regions, regulations, suppliers, and customer expectations, which adds layers of complexity.

TQM promotes a company-wide culture of quality, but implementing a TQM framework on a global scale can be challenging and resource-intensive, requiring alignment across cultures, regulations, and operational standards.

Lean and Kaizen are rooted in Japanese manufacturing practices, which may not translate seamlessly across different cultural and regulatory environments, further complicating their scalability in a global context.

Scaling traditional quality management practices across large, multinational organizations requires extensive training, coordination, and standardization, which can lead to inconsistencies, delays, and increased costs.

5. Difficulty in Integrating with Digital Systems and Technologies

One of the most significant challenges for traditional quality management approaches is the integration with digital systems and advanced technologies. With the rise of digital tools such as AI, machine learning, IoT, and cloud computing, organizations are increasingly relying on technology to streamline operations and enhance quality management.

Six Sigma and Lean are fundamentally process-oriented frameworks that are less adaptable to the integration of automated or AI-driven processes. Implementing digital tools alongside traditional methodologies often requires significant customization, investment, and training.

Traditional quality management tools, such as control charts or Pareto analysis, lack native compatibility with digital platforms that can offer automated quality monitoring and predictive insights.

In the digital age, organizations require quality management frameworks that can seamlessly integrate with various digital systems. Traditional approaches, however, often struggle to keep pace with digital advancements, creating barriers to optimizing quality processes through technology.

6. Challenges with Customer-Centric Quality in the Digital Era

Today's customers expect personalized, high-quality experiences at every interaction point. Traditional quality management approaches, however, often focus on internal processes rather than customer outcomes, which can lead to a misalignment between quality objectives and customer expectations.

TQM and Lean promote customer focus, but they often do so through indirect means, such as reducing defects or improving process efficiency, rather than directly measuring customer satisfaction.

In the digital age, organizations have access to customer data in real-time and can monitor customer feedback across multiple platforms. Traditional quality management approaches may not fully capitalize on these capabilities to deliver a truly customer-centric quality experience.

Incorporating customer feedback loops and real-time insights into quality management practices is essential in the digital age. Traditional approaches, however, may not emphasize customer experience to the same extent, leading to gaps in quality that impact customer satisfaction.

7. Focus on Incremental Improvement Rather Than Innovation

Traditional quality management methodologies emphasize continuous improvement, which typically focuses on incremental enhancements rather than breakthrough innovations. However, the digital age demands constant innovation to keep pace with competitors and meet rapidly evolving customer needs.

Kaizen and Lean methodologies prioritize small, incremental changes, which can limit an organization's ability to adopt bold, transformative changes.

Digital transformation, by contrast, often requires large-scale, disruptive innovations that go beyond incremental improvements. While continuous improvement remains important, organizations must also be prepared to undertake radical changes to remain competitive in the digital landscape.

Traditional approaches may inadvertently limit innovation by prioritizing minor improvements over radical, customer-driven advancements, potentially stalling digital transformation efforts.

The Need for Evolution in Quality Management

The digital age brings both challenges and opportunities for quality management. Traditional methodologies like Six Sigma, Lean, Kaizen, and TQM have established valuable foundations, yet they must evolve to meet the demands of modern digital environments. To remain effective, quality management must adapt by embracing data analytics, integrating with digital platforms, and fostering a customer-centric approach that prioritizes agility, real-time monitoring, and innovation.

Transitioning from traditional methods to a digital-first quality management strategy can help organizations maintain a competitive edge, align quality objectives with customer expectations, and address the unique challenges of today's complex, technology-driven world.

3. Digital Transformation and Its Impact on Quality Management

The advent of digital technologies has dramatically altered the way organizations operate, compete, and deliver value to their customers. Digital transformation, characterized by the integration of digital technologies into all areas of a business, fundamentally changes how organizations manage processes, including quality management. Quality management has traditionally focused on maintaining consistency and meeting established standards. However, in the digital age, quality management also involves leveraging data, connectivity, and smart systems to achieve real-time quality control, predictive analytics, and continuous improvement.

This chapter explores the scope and implications of digital transformation within quality management, examining how new technologies are reshaping traditional approaches and creating opportunities for more agile, efficient, and customer-focused quality practices.

3.1 Understanding Digital Transformation
Definition and Scope within Quality Management

Digital transformation in quality management refers to the strategic adoption of digital tools and technologies, such as the Internet of Things (IoT), artificial intelligence (AI), big data analytics, cloud computing, and smart systems, to improve quality processes, monitoring, and control. It encompasses more than just upgrading equipment or automating tasks; it's a shift in the organizational mindset, making technology a central enabler of quality, efficiency, and customer satisfaction.

The impact of digital transformation extends across the entire quality management landscape. It affects how quality data is collected, analyzed, and applied. Rather than relying solely on retrospective analysis, digital tools allow for real-time quality control and predictive insights. This allows organizations to prevent defects, respond immediately to quality issues, and maintain high standards consistently.

Key elements of digital transformation in quality management include:

Automation and Real-Time Monitoring: By automating quality checks and monitoring processes in real-time, digital technologies enable quicker identification of quality issues, reducing the time and cost associated with traditional quality inspection.

Data-Driven Decision Making: Access to vast amounts of data allows organizations to use analytics for better quality forecasting, predictive maintenance, and root cause analysis, leading to more proactive quality management.

Enhanced Customer-Centric Quality: Digital transformation allows for faster feedback loops with customers, enabling businesses to adapt quality measures based on real-time customer experiences and feedback.

Scalability and Flexibility: Digital tools facilitate easy scalability and adaptability, which are crucial for managing quality in rapidly changing and expanding business environments.

Role of Data, Connectivity, and Smart Systems

Digital transformation hinges on three core components—data, connectivity, and smart systems—that revolutionize quality management practices.

1. Data as the Foundation of Digital Quality Management

Data is at the heart of digital transformation in quality management. Quality metrics and data insights enable a transition from reactive quality control (QC) to proactive and predictive quality management, where data can be leveraged for continual improvement and long-term planning.

Big Data Analytics: The rise of big data technologies allows organizations to process large volumes of information from multiple sources, including customer feedback, supplier data, and operational metrics. This enables the detection of patterns that might not be evident in smaller, isolated datasets.

Predictive Analytics: Data collected over time can be used to forecast quality issues before they arise. Predictive analytics helps companies anticipate defects, optimize maintenance schedules, and reduce downtime, thus improving product quality and customer satisfaction.

Machine Learning and AI: Machine learning algorithms can analyze quality-related data and provide insights into improvement areas. For instance, AI can detect anomalies, recognize patterns, and make recommendations based on historical data, aiding decision-makers in preventing recurring quality issues.

The shift towards a data-driven approach not only improves the accuracy of quality management but also enables more strategic decisions, helping organizations to align quality objectives with broader business goals.

2. Connectivity: The Internet of Things (IoT) and Quality Management

The Internet of Things (IoT) brings a new level of connectivity to quality management. By embedding sensors and communication devices in equipment, IoT enables continuous monitoring and real-time data transmission. IoT has several implications for quality management:

Real-Time Quality Monitoring: IoT sensors can continuously monitor various quality parameters, such as temperature, pressure, and humidity, that might affect product quality. This allows companies to detect quality issues in real time and make immediate adjustments to maintain standards.

Preventive Maintenance and Reduced Downtime: IoT-enabled systems can track equipment conditions and performance, predicting when maintenance is required. Preventive maintenance reduces equipment failure and downtime, which are common causes of quality issues.

Enhanced Supply Chain Visibility: IoT technology improves supply chain traceability, allowing organizations to track the quality of materials and components throughout the supply chain. This visibility helps in identifying potential quality risks early, ensuring that only high-quality materials reach production.

By connecting devices, machines, and systems, IoT facilitates a seamless flow of information, enabling a holistic view of quality across the production process. This interconnectedness ensures that each part of the production chain meets quality standards, reducing defects and increasing consistency.

3. Smart Systems: AI, Automation, and Robotics in Quality Management

Smart systems, powered by AI, robotics, and automation, play a vital role in advancing quality management processes. These systems allow for automated quality control, data analysis, and real-time feedback, transforming how quality is managed in modern organizations.

Automated Quality Control: Robotics and automation enable repetitive quality checks to be carried out consistently and accurately. For instance, automated visual inspection systems can detect minute defects in products with greater precision than human inspectors.

AI-Powered Quality Analytics: AI can analyze data from various sources to identify trends, patterns, and outliers. It can also recommend improvements, streamline quality processes, and even automate certain quality-related decisions, such as flagging defective products or adjusting production parameters.

Intelligent Process Control: AI and machine learning can continuously adjust process parameters based on real-time data to ensure that quality remains within specified limits. This self-regulating capability is particularly useful in industries like manufacturing, where minor deviations in process parameters can significantly impact product quality.

By integrating smart systems into quality management, organizations can achieve higher levels of accuracy, reduce human error, and ensure that quality standards are consistently met.

Benefits of Digital Transformation in Quality Management

Digital transformation offers several advantages that directly impact the quality of products and services. Some of the key benefits include:

Increased Efficiency: Automated and data-driven processes reduce manual tasks, streamline workflows, and allow for more efficient use of resources, reducing costs and improving productivity.

Enhanced Accuracy and Consistency: Digital tools and automated systems minimize human error and ensure a higher degree of consistency in quality checks.

Proactive Quality Management: With predictive analytics and real-time monitoring, organizations can identify and address potential quality issues before they affect the customer, ensuring proactive quality management.

Customer-Centric Quality Focus: Digital transformation enables organizations to collect real-time feedback from customers, allowing them to adapt quality measures based on actual customer experience.

Scalability and Flexibility: Digital tools allow quality management practices to scale and adapt as organizations grow or enter new markets, making it easier to maintain high quality across diverse operations and geographies.

Digital transformation is reshaping quality management, enabling organizations to transition from traditional, reactive quality approaches to proactive, predictive, and data-driven quality management. By leveraging data, connectivity, and smart systems, companies can achieve unprecedented levels of quality control, customer satisfaction, and operational efficiency. As quality management becomes increasingly digital, organizations are better positioned to meet the demands of a rapidly evolving market, maintaining a competitive edge and delivering products that consistently meet or exceed customer expectations.

3.2 Key Benefits of Digital Transformation for Quality

The adoption of digital transformation in quality management has brought about profound changes, enhancing the way organizations approach, maintain, and improve quality across all levels. Digital tools and technologies have enabled a shift from traditional, manual, and often fragmented quality processes to more streamlined, integrated, and responsive approaches. This section explores how digital transformation specifically contributes to enhanced accuracy, speed, and responsiveness in quality processes, ultimately helping organizations deliver better products, increase efficiency, and stay competitive in rapidly changing markets.

Enhanced Accuracy in Quality Processes

Accuracy is foundational to quality management. A high level of accuracy ensures that products meet specified standards, customer expectations, and regulatory requirements. Digital transformation enhances accuracy by introducing automation, real-time data analytics, and AI-driven insights, which reduce human error and allow for a more precise approach to quality management.

Automation and Reduced Human Error: Automation of routine quality tasks, such as inspections, measurements, and reporting, drastically reduces the margin for human error. In manual processes, even small lapses in attention or consistency can lead to significant quality deviations, which could affect customer satisfaction and compliance. Automated systems carry out these tasks with precision, producing consistent results each time. For example, automated visual inspection systems can detect even the smallest defects in manufactured products, which may be difficult for human inspectors to identify consistently. These systems also function with a higher degree of repeatability, ensuring that each product is inspected to the same standard, which elevates overall accuracy.

Real-Time Data Collection and Analysis: Digital technologies allow organizations to collect and analyze data in real time, a critical component in maintaining accuracy throughout the production process. Real-time data collection enables the immediate identification of variations or anomalies, allowing for quick corrective actions before the issue escalates or impacts a significant portion of the production batch. This real-time insight into quality metrics ensures that organizations maintain accuracy continuously and consistently, aligning with both internal standards and external regulatory requirements.

AI-Driven Quality Analysis: Artificial Intelligence (AI) plays a key role in enhancing accuracy by identifying patterns and insights within vast datasets that would be challenging to detect manually. Machine learning algorithms can predict potential quality issues based on historical data and recognize trends that might indicate a problem before it arises. For instance, predictive maintenance can identify when equipment is likely to fail or produce off-spec products, allowing quality managers to intervene before issues occur. Additionally, AI can process complex datasets more accurately than manual or even traditional statistical methods, providing a highly reliable basis for decision-making.

IoT-Enabled Precision: The Internet of Things (IoT) contributes to accuracy in quality management by facilitating precise monitoring and control over production parameters. IoT-enabled sensors collect data on various production factors—such as temperature, pressure, and humidity—that can affect product quality. This precise control over production parameters ensures that each product is manufactured under optimal conditions, thereby increasing consistency and accuracy. Moreover, IoT devices transmit data in real-time, enabling organizations to adjust parameters instantly to correct any deviations from the desired quality standards.

Increased Speed in Quality Processes

Speed is a critical aspect of modern quality management, particularly as customer expectations for rapid service and high-quality products continue to rise. Digital transformation enhances the speed of quality processes through automation, real-time analytics, and advanced communication technologies, allowing organizations to maintain quality without compromising on time.

Automated Inspections and Testing: Automation accelerates quality processes by performing inspections, measurements, and testing at a pace far beyond human capabilities. Automated visual inspection systems, for example, can scan thousands of parts per minute for defects, a task that would be impossible for human inspectors to complete with the same speed or precision. These systems also reduce the time spent on repetitive tasks, allowing quality teams to focus on more complex issues, ultimately speeding up the overall quality process.

Real-Time Quality Control and Adjustment: The ability to monitor and adjust quality metrics in real time has transformed quality control. Previously, quality checks were often conducted after the fact, meaning any detected issues had already affected a batch of products. Real-time control, enabled by digital tools and IoT sensors, allows quality teams to monitor production continuously and make instant adjustments if quality begins to deviate from standards. This capability reduces the time needed for rework or recalls, as issues can be addressed immediately before they escalate.

AI and Machine Learning for Faster Decision-Making: AI and machine learning enable faster decision-making in quality management by processing data rapidly and identifying solutions in a fraction of the time required for manual analysis. For example, machine learning algorithms can analyze defect patterns, identify probable causes, and suggest corrective actions within seconds. This ability to expedite decision-making is essential in high-volume production environments, where even a brief delay in addressing quality issues can lead to significant losses. Moreover, AI-driven predictive insights allow organizations to proactively address potential issues, further reducing time spent on quality control.

Improved Communication and Coordination: Digital transformation facilitates quicker communication across departments and between supply chain partners, which is essential in ensuring that quality standards are upheld throughout the production process. For instance, a quality issue identified by IoT sensors on the production floor can trigger an automatic notification to relevant teams, prompting immediate corrective action. This real-time communication reduces delays in identifying and addressing quality issues, resulting in faster resolutions and an overall improvement in quality speed.

Enhanced Responsiveness in Quality Management

Responsiveness is crucial in today's fast-paced business environment, where companies must be agile and capable of addressing quality issues swiftly to maintain customer satisfaction and competitive advantage. Digital transformation improves responsiveness in quality management by enabling proactive and predictive capabilities, fostering a more agile and adaptable approach to quality challenges.

Predictive Maintenance and Quality Control: Digital tools, particularly those powered by IoT and AI, allow organizations to move from reactive to predictive maintenance. Rather than waiting for quality issues to occur, predictive maintenance enables quality teams to anticipate potential equipment failures and take preemptive action. This shift significantly reduces downtime and prevents quality issues from reaching the customer. Predictive maintenance also improves responsiveness by minimizing unexpected disruptions, which can compromise both production speed and quality.

Rapid Problem Identification and Root Cause Analysis: Digital technologies enable rapid identification of quality issues, often before they affect the final product. For example, machine learning algorithms can analyze real-time data to detect deviations that could indicate potential quality problems. Furthermore, AI-powered root cause analysis tools can quickly identify the underlying causes of quality issues, allowing for faster implementation of corrective actions. This rapid problem identification ensures that quality issues are addressed in real time, minimizing their impact and allowing for a more responsive quality management process.

Agility in Adapting to Changing Standards and Customer Expectations: In today's competitive landscape, customer expectations and regulatory standards evolve rapidly. Digital transformation allows quality management systems to adapt swiftly to these changes. For instance, cloud-based quality management systems can be updated remotely to meet new standards or requirements, enabling organizations to maintain compliance without interrupting operations. Additionally, digital tools facilitate the quick analysis of customer feedback, enabling quality teams to make immediate adjustments to meet customer needs.

Enhanced Traceability and Supply Chain Responsiveness: Digital transformation enhances traceability within the supply chain, allowing organizations to quickly trace quality issues to their sources. IoT and blockchain technologies, for example, offer end-to-end visibility into the supply chain, making it easier to identify where quality issues originate, whether in raw materials, manufacturing, or logistics. This traceability enhances responsiveness by allowing organizations to isolate and resolve quality problems more quickly, preventing them from affecting subsequent stages of the production process.

Continuous Improvement and Real-Time Feedback Loops: Digital tools facilitate continuous improvement by enabling real-time feedback loops in quality processes. For example, data from IoT sensors can be fed directly into analytics platforms that provide ongoing insights into quality performance. These insights can inform continuous improvement initiatives, allowing organizations to respond dynamically to new quality challenges as they arise. By fostering a culture of continuous improvement, digital transformation ensures that quality management processes remain responsive to changes in production environments, customer expectations, and industry standards.

Digital transformation has revolutionized quality management by enhancing accuracy, speed, and responsiveness. Automated systems and AI-driven insights reduce human error and improve consistency in quality checks, ensuring that products meet or exceed quality standards. Real-time monitoring and rapid decision-making increase the speed of quality processes, enabling organizations to maintain high standards without sacrificing efficiency. Enhanced responsiveness, supported by predictive maintenance, rapid root cause analysis, and agile adaptation to changing requirements, ensures that quality issues are addressed promptly, minimizing their impact on customers and production.

As businesses continue to adopt digital tools and technologies, quality management will become increasingly proactive, data-driven, and adaptable, positioning organizations to thrive in a dynamic and competitive landscape. Digital transformation thus empowers companies to deliver consistent, high-quality products and services that align with the evolving demands of modern consumers, driving sustained success and customer loyalty.

3.3 Key Challenges of Digital Transformation for Quality Management

While digital transformation presents significant benefits for quality management, it also brings several challenges that organizations must address to succeed. These challenges, which include managing organizational change, technology adoption hurdles, bridging skills gaps, and ensuring data privacy, can slow down or even hinder the digital transformation process if not properly managed. This section examines these challenges in detail, exploring their impact on quality management and offering insights into potential strategies to overcome them.

1. Change Management in Digital Transformation

One of the most pressing challenges in digital transformation for quality management is change management. Implementing new technologies and processes often disrupts established routines, requiring organizations to adopt new approaches and attitudes toward work. Resistance to change, lack of buy-in from stakeholders, and a lack of clear communication around the transformation objectives can make it difficult to integrate digital practices effectively.

Resistance to Change: Employees and management teams accustomed to traditional methods may resist the adoption of new digital tools. This resistance can arise from fear of the unknown, concerns about job security, or discomfort with learning new systems. For instance, workers who have been inspecting products manually for years may resist transitioning to automated inspection systems, fearing that the technology might replace their roles or undermine their expertise. Overcoming this resistance requires creating an environment where employees understand the benefits of digital transformation and feel that they are part of the transition rather than replaced by it.

Need for Strong Leadership and Clear Communication: Effective change management depends on strong leadership and clear communication. Leaders play a critical role in motivating and guiding teams through the transformation process. By articulating a clear vision of how digital transformation will improve quality management and benefit employees and customers, leaders can generate buy-in from all levels of the organization. Regular updates, open forums for feedback, and hands-on demonstrations of new technologies can further support employees in adapting to the changes.

Cultural Shift Towards Innovation: Digital transformation requires a cultural shift where innovation, agility, and continuous improvement become central values. Building such a culture may require redefining company values, revising incentive structures, and providing ongoing education on the importance of digital transformation. Organizations that foster a culture that embraces change, innovation, and continuous improvement find it easier to implement and sustain digital transformation in quality management.

2. Technology Adoption and Integration

The rapid evolution of digital technologies brings unique challenges in terms of selecting, adopting, and integrating new tools and platforms into quality management systems. Many organizations struggle with the high costs, complex integrations, and constant updates required for digital transformation.

High Costs of Implementation: Implementing digital quality management solutions, such as AI-driven analytics, IoT sensors, or automated inspection systems, often requires significant financial investment. Organizations, especially small and medium-sized enterprises (SMEs), may struggle to justify these costs. Furthermore, achieving a return on investment (ROI) from these technologies can take time, which may cause hesitation in adopting digital tools that appear to carry high upfront costs. To address this challenge, organizations must conduct thorough cost-benefit analyses and consider phased approaches to implementation, focusing on high-impact areas that can yield quicker returns.

Complexity of System Integration: The integration of new digital tools with existing systems presents another challenge. Quality management typically relies on multiple platforms, such as ERP (Enterprise Resource Planning), MES (Manufacturing Execution Systems), and legacy systems. Ensuring that new digital tools are compatible with these existing systems requires significant time, expertise, and resources.

For example, integrating IoT devices to monitor production parameters with legacy software can require custom solutions, specialized skills, and careful planning to prevent data silos and maximize data interoperability.

Frequent Updates and Upgrades: Technology evolves rapidly, and digital tools used for quality management are no exception. Frequent updates and upgrades are often necessary to maintain optimal performance, improve security, and stay aligned with the latest standards. However, managing these updates can be challenging, as it requires continuous learning and adaptation by employees and may occasionally disrupt quality processes. Organizations need to allocate resources for regular maintenance and ensure that staff receive ongoing training to stay up-to-date with evolving technologies.

3. Skills Gap and Workforce Readiness

Digital transformation in quality management demands new technical and analytical skills that are often not present within the existing workforce. Bridging this skills gap is crucial for successful implementation and sustainability of digital quality management practices.

Lack of Technical Expertise: Digital quality management requires skills in areas such as data analytics, machine learning, and IoT operations, which may not be part of the existing skill set of many quality professionals. For example, quality inspectors who previously relied on manual processes may struggle to interpret complex data visualizations or operate automated systems without proper training. To address this skills gap, organizations need to invest in targeted training programs and consider hiring specialists with the required technical skills.

Retraining and Upskilling Initiatives: Upskilling current employees and preparing them for the digital aspects of quality management is critical. Retraining initiatives can focus on specific skills, such as data interpretation, software navigation, or equipment operation. Additionally, organizations can offer certifications or partner with training institutions to provide employees with comprehensive digital training. By prioritizing workforce development, organizations can bridge the skills gap and prepare their teams to embrace and excel in digital transformation.

Addressing the Shortage of Qualified Talent: There is often a shortage of qualified talent with expertise in both digital technologies and quality management principles. This shortage can hinder an organization's ability to implement and maintain digital quality management practices effectively. To attract such talent, organizations may need to consider competitive compensation packages, career development opportunities, and flexible work options. Building a pipeline of digitally skilled quality professionals through internships, apprenticeships, or partnerships with educational institutions can also help in addressing the talent gap over the long term.

4. Data Privacy and Security

As organizations increasingly rely on data to drive quality decisions, protecting sensitive information and maintaining customer trust becomes a paramount concern. Data privacy and security are especially important in quality management, where data collection and analysis often involve proprietary information, customer data, and regulatory requirements.

Protecting Sensitive Quality Data: Digital quality management systems often involve collecting and storing data related to products, processes, and customer preferences. This information is valuable for making quality decisions but can be sensitive if it includes proprietary details or customer-specific data. Ensuring that data is securely stored, transmitted, and accessed is essential to prevent unauthorized access, breaches, and data leaks. Organizations need to implement robust data security protocols, such as encryption, access controls, and regular audits, to protect this information.

Compliance with Data Privacy Regulations: Compliance with data privacy regulations, such as GDPR (General Data Protection Regulation) in Europe or CCPA (California Consumer Privacy Act) in the United States, is a significant challenge for organizations engaged in digital transformation. These regulations mandate strict controls over how data is collected, stored, and shared, and organizations face significant fines for non-compliance. To adhere to these regulations, organizations must establish clear data privacy policies, provide training to employees on data handling practices, and ensure that their digital quality management systems comply with applicable legal requirements.

Risk of Cyberattacks: As quality management systems become digitized and connected to the internet, they become potential targets for cyberattacks. Hackers may attempt to exploit vulnerabilities in IoT devices, cloud platforms, or software systems to gain unauthorized access or disrupt quality processes. A cyberattack could not only compromise sensitive quality data but also disrupt production, resulting in delays and financial losses. Organizations must prioritize cybersecurity measures, such as firewalls, intrusion detection systems, and regular vulnerability assessments, to protect their quality management systems from potential threats.

Balancing Data Access and Privacy Needs: While data is essential for driving quality improvements, balancing data access with privacy needs can be challenging. Quality teams require access to detailed, real-time data to make effective decisions, but unrestricted access to data increases the risk of privacy violations. Implementing role-based access controls, anonymizing sensitive data where possible, and establishing clear guidelines for data access can help organizations strike a balance between data availability and privacy protection.

The journey toward digital transformation in quality management is laden with challenges, but by addressing these issues proactively, organizations can unlock the full potential of digital tools and processes. Change management requires a cultural shift and strong leadership to overcome resistance and foster a positive attitude toward digital adoption. Successfully integrating new technologies demands careful planning and a willingness to invest in the necessary resources, while bridging the skills gap involves comprehensive training and workforce development programs. Finally, ensuring data privacy and security is essential to maintain customer trust and protect sensitive information in an increasingly interconnected environment.

By embracing a strategic approach to these challenges, organizations can build a resilient digital quality management framework that not only improves product quality and operational efficiency but also strengthens their competitive position in an ever-evolving market.

4. Emerging Technologies in Quality Management

As industries become increasingly digitized, emerging technologies are reshaping quality management by introducing new capabilities for precision, efficiency, and strategic insight. Among these technologies, Artificial Intelligence (AI) and Machine Learning (ML) stand out for their potential to revolutionize traditional quality practices, offering unprecedented tools to improve quality control, enhance predictive maintenance, and support proactive decision-making. This section explores these technologies, examining how they function in quality management, their various applications, and the specific benefits they bring.

4.1 Artificial Intelligence and Machine Learning

Artificial Intelligence and Machine Learning are two foundational pillars driving digital transformation in quality management. While both terms are often used interchangeably, they have distinct meanings. AI refers to the simulation of human intelligence in machines, enabling them to perform tasks such as problem-solving, decision-making, and language understanding. Machine Learning, a subset of AI, refers to the ability of machines to learn from data and improve their performance over time without explicit programming. In quality management, these technologies enable powerful insights into quality processes, support predictive maintenance, and help identify defects before they impact production.

AI-Driven Insights for Quality Improvement and Predictive Maintenance

AI-driven insights transform quality management by enabling data analysis at a scale and depth that was previously unattainable. By applying advanced algorithms to large datasets, AI systems can uncover hidden patterns, predict potential issues, and suggest corrective actions.

In particular, AI is instrumental in predictive maintenance, helping organizations identify potential equipment failures before they occur.

Enhancing Quality Control with Data Analysis: AI can analyze vast amounts of data from production processes to detect anomalies that might indicate quality issues. In a production line, various sensors collect data on factors such as temperature, humidity, pressure, and machine performance. AI algorithms can analyze this data in real-time, alerting quality managers to any deviations from optimal conditions that might compromise product quality. This real-time analysis allows for quick adjustments, reducing the likelihood of defective products and minimizing waste.

Predictive Maintenance: Predictive maintenance is one of the most impactful applications of AI in quality management. Traditional maintenance strategies, such as preventive or reactive maintenance, often lead to inefficiencies and costly downtimes. In contrast, predictive maintenance leverages AI to anticipate when machinery will likely require servicing. By continuously monitoring equipment data—such as vibration patterns, noise levels, and temperature—AI algorithms can predict potential failures. This proactive approach not only prevents unexpected breakdowns but also optimizes maintenance schedules, reducing downtime and extending the lifespan of machinery. As a result, companies can ensure that their production processes run smoothly, maintaining consistent quality and minimizing disruptions.

Automated Root Cause Analysis: Identifying the root causes of quality issues can be a time-consuming task, particularly in complex production environments with multiple variables. AI algorithms are highly effective in automating root cause analysis, using pattern recognition and anomaly detection to pinpoint specific issues. For example, if a manufacturing plant notices an increase in defective products, AI can analyze data from across the production line to identify the cause—whether it's a machine malfunction, incorrect raw material specifications, or a change in environmental conditions. This automated approach to root cause analysis allows for quicker responses to quality issues, reducing product recalls and safeguarding brand reputation.

Improving Quality Forecasting: Quality forecasting is essential for planning and resource allocation. AI-driven forecasting models can help quality managers anticipate fluctuations in quality based on historical data and external factors such as supplier quality, seasonality, and demand patterns. For example, AI can analyze data trends to predict seasonal variations in product quality, enabling managers to allocate resources more effectively and take proactive steps to prevent quality issues.

Enhancing Customer Feedback Analysis: AI also supports quality improvement by analyzing customer feedback, a critical but often underutilized data source. Natural Language Processing (NLP), a subset of AI, can sift through large volumes of customer reviews, social media posts, and support tickets to extract insights about customer satisfaction and product quality. By identifying recurring complaints, AI helps quality managers prioritize areas for improvement and ensure that future products align better with customer expectations.

Applications of Machine Learning in Defect Detection and Quality Forecasting

Machine Learning plays a pivotal role in defect detection and quality forecasting, two areas critical to maintaining high-quality standards in production. By learning from historical data and improving over time, ML models offer continuous enhancements in accuracy, enabling organizations to detect defects early and forecast quality trends effectively.

Automated Defect Detection: Traditional methods of defect detection rely on manual inspection or rule-based systems, both of which are prone to errors and inefficiencies. ML algorithms, particularly in the field of computer vision, have transformed defect detection by enabling automated and highly accurate visual inspections. Using cameras and ML models trained on thousands of images, these systems can identify even the smallest defects that might go unnoticed by human inspectors.

For instance, in electronics manufacturing, ML-based image recognition systems can detect microscopic soldering errors on circuit boards. In automotive manufacturing, similar systems can inspect car parts for surface defects such as scratches, dents, or uneven paint applications. The precision of ML in defect detection not only reduces the likelihood of defective products reaching customers but also frees up human inspectors to focus on more complex tasks, enhancing productivity and overall quality.

Real-Time Quality Monitoring: Machine Learning models can monitor quality in real time by analyzing data from production lines as it is generated. For example, an ML system could monitor the viscosity of a liquid during a mixing process, alerting operators if the viscosity deviates from the optimal range, which might indicate an issue with raw materials or mixing conditions. This real-time monitoring capability enables immediate corrective actions, minimizing the number of defective products and reducing waste.

Anomaly Detection for Early Issue Identification: ML excels at anomaly detection, which is particularly valuable in identifying subtle, non-obvious defects that may escape conventional inspection methods. By analyzing patterns in historical data, ML algorithms can detect outliers that indicate potential quality issues. For instance, in a pharmaceutical manufacturing process, slight deviations in mixing times or temperatures might affect product quality. Anomaly detection can flag these deviations early, allowing for corrective action before products reach consumers.

Quality Forecasting and Demand Prediction: ML algorithms are highly effective in forecasting quality trends by analyzing historical data, seasonal factors, and external variables. This capability is valuable in industries where quality may fluctuate based on environmental conditions, demand spikes, or supply chain variability. By accurately forecasting quality trends, organizations can adjust production parameters, allocate resources effectively, and prepare for potential quality issues before they arise.

Customized Quality Control Processes: ML can support customized quality control processes by analyzing data specific to each product line or production batch. For instance, a factory producing various types of beverages can use ML to analyze the unique quality parameters for each product. This customization allows for more precise quality control, as ML models are tailored to the specific characteristics of each product, reducing variability and improving overall quality.

Predictive Models for Supplier Quality Management: Quality management often extends beyond internal processes to include suppliers, whose quality levels directly impact the final product. ML can analyze supplier data to predict potential quality issues, enabling organizations to address these issues proactively. For example, if a supplier consistently delivers raw materials with slight variations, ML models can predict how these variations will affect production quality. Armed with these insights, organizations can work closely with suppliers to meet quality standards, enhancing consistency and reducing the risk of defective products.

Adaptive Quality Control through Reinforcement Learning: Reinforcement Learning (RL), an advanced branch of ML, enables adaptive quality control by allowing machines to learn from their actions and optimize their responses over time. In a quality management context, RL systems can adjust production parameters automatically based on real-time feedback, optimizing quality continuously. For example, an RL system in a chemical manufacturing process could adjust mixing times, temperatures, and ingredient ratios in real time to achieve the best possible product quality. This adaptive approach not only enhances quality but also improves efficiency, as adjustments are made dynamically to match current conditions.

Challenges of Implementing AI and ML in Quality Management

While AI and ML offer substantial benefits, they also present implementation challenges that organizations must navigate to succeed.

Data Quality and Quantity: Effective ML models require large, high-quality datasets. Collecting and organizing sufficient data can be challenging, particularly for organizations new to digital transformation.

Inconsistent or incomplete data can lead to inaccurate predictions, limiting the effectiveness of AI-driven quality management.

Integration with Existing Systems: AI and ML systems must integrate seamlessly with existing quality management tools and production systems, which can be complex and costly. Ensuring compatibility across multiple platforms and data sources requires careful planning and technical expertise.

Skill Gaps and Training Needs: Implementing AI-driven quality management systems requires specialized skills in data science, machine learning, and AI technologies. Many organizations face a shortage of these skills, necessitating training programs or external hiring to build a capable workforce.

Data Privacy and Security Concerns: AI systems often rely on sensitive data, raising concerns around data privacy and security. Ensuring that data is stored and processed securely is essential to maintain customer trust and meet regulatory requirements.

Cost and ROI Considerations: While AI and ML offer long-term benefits, the initial investment can be substantial. Organizations must balance the costs of implementation with the anticipated return on investment, which may take time to realize fully.

The integration of Artificial Intelligence and Machine Learning in quality management is a transformative shift that empowers organizations to enhance precision, predict quality issues, and optimize processes in ways previously unimaginable. By harnessing AI-driven insights for predictive maintenance and leveraging ML for defect detection and quality forecasting, organizations can improve product quality, reduce waste, and increase customer satisfaction. Although there are challenges, such as data requirements, skills gaps, and integration complexities, the long-term benefits of adopting these technologies make them a critical asset in the digital age of quality management.

4.2 Internet of Things (IoT) and Smart Sensors

As manufacturing and production environments embrace digital transformation, the Internet of Things (IoT) and smart sensors are emerging as indispensable tools in modern quality management. IoT enables interconnectivity between devices, machines, and systems, facilitating real-time data collection and transmission across various points of a production line. Smart sensors, a crucial component of IoT, gather and transmit real-time information about process conditions, machine status, environmental factors, and product quality metrics. These innovations have opened new avenues for real-time quality monitoring and automated data collection, empowering businesses to make data-driven decisions, anticipate quality issues, and optimize their processes.

Real-Time Quality Monitoring Using IoT

Real-time quality monitoring is one of the most impactful benefits IoT brings to quality management. In a connected IoT environment, data is gathered from various points in the production process and immediately processed to detect any deviations from quality standards. This ability to monitor quality in real-time is instrumental in maintaining consistent product standards, identifying emerging issues, and ensuring operational efficiency.

Continuous Process Monitoring: With IoT-enabled systems, manufacturers can monitor every aspect of the production process as it happens. For instance, in a pharmaceutical production line, IoT devices can track and record conditions such as temperature, humidity, and pressure, which are critical for product quality. If any of these factors deviates from the acceptable range, the system can alert operators to address the issue promptly. This proactive approach ensures that products maintain consistent quality without requiring extensive manual intervention.

Immediate Detection of Quality Defects: IoT systems can detect quality defects in real-time, allowing for immediate corrective actions. For example, if a machine malfunctions and starts producing defective products, IoT sensors can detect unusual patterns in vibration, temperature, or product dimensions. This information is then sent to a central system that alerts quality managers, enabling them to halt production, conduct inspections, and resolve the issue before a large batch of defective products is produced. This real-time defect detection reduces waste, improves operational efficiency, and prevents defective products from reaching customers.

Remote Monitoring and Control: IoT enables remote monitoring and control of quality parameters, which is particularly useful for organizations with distributed manufacturing operations. Quality managers can access real-time data from any location, allowing them to oversee production lines in different facilities. This ability to monitor processes remotely enhances flexibility and response times, enabling swift interventions when necessary. Additionally, managers can adjust process settings remotely, such as changing machine parameters or calibrating sensors, ensuring continuous quality compliance across all locations.

Predictive Quality Management: The combination of IoT and data analytics facilitates predictive quality management, where potential quality issues are identified before they become critical. By analyzing historical data from IoT sensors, manufacturers can recognize patterns that indicate potential failures or deviations from quality standards. This predictive capability allows them to address issues proactively, reducing downtime, minimizing waste, and ensuring products meet quality standards. For instance, if sensor data reveals a gradual increase in machine temperature, it may indicate a need for maintenance, which can be scheduled before quality is compromised.

Quality Data Centralization and Real-Time Dashboards: IoT supports the centralization of quality data from multiple production lines, enabling quality managers to access all relevant information through a single dashboard. This centralized view is invaluable for decision-making, as it provides real-time insights into production performance, quality metrics, and areas requiring attention. Real-time dashboards can display key performance indicators (KPIs) such as defect rates, process efficiency, and compliance with quality standards. This visibility allows managers to make informed decisions, optimize resource allocation, and prioritize areas that need improvement.

Smart Sensors for Data Collection on Production Lines

Smart sensors are the foundation of IoT-enabled quality management. They continuously monitor various aspects of production, collecting data on everything from machine performance to environmental conditions. These sensors enable precision, consistency, and automated adjustments that traditional quality management methods often struggle to achieve.

Types of Smart Sensors and Their Applications: Smart sensors come in various forms, each designed to monitor specific conditions essential to product quality. Common types include:

Temperature Sensors: Monitor temperature to ensure products are produced under optimal conditions, which is especially critical in industries like food, pharmaceuticals, and electronics.

Humidity Sensors: Used to monitor moisture levels, which can affect product quality in sectors such as pharmaceuticals and food processing.

Vibration Sensors: Detect mechanical issues in equipment by analyzing vibration patterns, which can indicate wear and tear, misalignment, or other faults.

Optical and Vision Sensors: Used for visual inspections, such as checking product dimensions, surface defects, and color consistency, to ensure products meet specifications.

Pressure Sensors: Measure pressure in production environments where precise pressure levels are essential for product quality, such as in the automotive and aerospace industries.

These sensors provide accurate, real-time data that helps maintain consistent quality, detect deviations, and prevent defects.

Enhanced Data Collection and Accuracy: Traditional quality checks often rely on manual data collection, which can be time-consuming and prone to human error. Smart sensors automate data collection, capturing vast amounts of information with precision and accuracy. For example, in a chemical manufacturing plant, sensors can continuously monitor and record the exact concentration of ingredients in a mixture, ensuring that each batch meets the required specifications. This automation not only improves data accuracy but also frees up personnel to focus on higher-level quality management tasks.

Data-Driven Process Optimization: With the data collected by smart sensors, manufacturers can analyze their production processes and identify opportunities for optimization. For instance, if sensors reveal that certain machines consistently operate below optimal performance levels, maintenance schedules can be adjusted to improve efficiency and prevent future breakdowns. In this way, data-driven process optimization helps to refine the production line, reduce downtime, and maintain consistent product quality. Through continuous data analysis, manufacturers can optimize workflows, eliminate bottlenecks, and fine-tune processes to achieve greater efficiency and quality standards.

Automated Quality Control and Inspection: Smart sensors facilitate automated quality control, reducing reliance on manual inspections. By integrating sensors directly into production machinery, companies can achieve real-time, automated checks at each stage of production. For example, vision sensors can scan products on an assembly line, immediately identifying any defects such as surface irregularities or size inconsistencies. This level of automation not only speeds up quality checks but also ensures that only compliant products proceed to the next stage, significantly reducing the risk of defective goods reaching customers.

Real-Time Feedback and Adaptive Control: One of the significant advantages of smart sensors is their ability to provide real-time feedback to machines and systems, allowing for adaptive control. When a sensor detects a deviation, it can send an immediate signal to adjust settings, ensuring the process remains within desired quality parameters. For instance, if a temperature sensor detects a rise in oven temperature in a food production line, it can trigger an automatic adjustment to bring it back within the safe range. This adaptive control minimizes the likelihood of quality issues and contributes to a more stable production environment.

Reducing Wastage and Enhancing Sustainability: By continuously monitoring quality metrics and ensuring process adherence, smart sensors help reduce material waste. Since quality issues are detected and addressed immediately, fewer defective products are produced, leading to less rework and waste disposal. This contributes to sustainability goals by lowering resource consumption and reducing the environmental impact of manufacturing processes. In industries with strict environmental standards, such as automotive or electronics manufacturing, minimizing waste through precise quality control is crucial for regulatory compliance and cost savings.

Data Archiving for Compliance and Traceability: Quality management systems integrated with IoT sensors enable comprehensive data archiving, creating a historical record of production data that is valuable for compliance and traceability. For regulated industries, such as pharmaceuticals and aerospace, having an accurate, detailed record of production parameters is essential for meeting industry standards and facilitating audits. If a defect is discovered after production, archived data can trace back through every stage, helping to identify root causes and implement corrective measures. This enhances accountability, compliance, and the ability to address issues efficiently.

Challenges and Considerations in Implementing IoT and Smart Sensors in Quality Management

While IoT and smart sensors offer significant benefits to quality management, their integration into production environments also presents some challenges.

Cost of Implementation and Maintenance: Installing IoT infrastructure and smart sensors requires an upfront investment in hardware, software, and network systems. The costs include purchasing sensors, upgrading machinery, and implementing network connections, which can be substantial. Additionally, maintenance of IoT systems, particularly for calibration and sensor replacements, must be factored into operational budgets.

Data Security and Privacy Concerns: IoT systems collect vast amounts of data, some of which may be sensitive. Ensuring data security is essential to protect proprietary information and customer privacy. Manufacturers need robust cybersecurity measures, including encryption, secure data storage, and regular security audits, to prevent unauthorized access to IoT systems. As production data often flows between multiple systems, maintaining secure data transmission is critical to prevent cyber threats from compromising quality management processes.

Integration with Existing Systems: Integrating IoT technology with existing manufacturing infrastructure can be complex, especially for older equipment. Achieving seamless interoperability between traditional machinery and IoT systems often requires custom integration or retrofitting of machines with compatible sensors. This integration process may involve technical expertise and can be time-intensive, but it is necessary for ensuring that IoT solutions operate effectively within current production lines.

Data Overload and Analytical Challenges: IoT-enabled sensors can generate enormous volumes of data, leading to potential data overload. Without effective data management and analysis capabilities, this information may be challenging to process and interpret. Manufacturers need advanced data analytics tools and personnel with expertise in data science to extract actionable insights from sensor data. Investing in machine learning and AI-powered analytics can help transform raw data into meaningful quality improvements, but this requires both technical resources and a strategic approach to data management.

Skills Gap and Workforce Training: Introducing IoT and smart sensors requires skilled personnel to manage, maintain, and interpret data generated by these technologies. Many organizations face a skills gap, as their current workforce may lack experience with digital tools and IoT devices. To maximize the benefits of IoT-based quality management, companies must invest in training programs to upskill their employees in areas such as data analysis, sensor calibration, and system troubleshooting.

Future of IoT and Smart Sensors in Quality Management

The adoption of IoT and smart sensors is rapidly reshaping the landscape of quality management, with new advancements continuously emerging. As IoT technology evolves, so does its potential for quality management innovations.

Integration with Artificial Intelligence for Advanced Insights: The future of IoT in quality management is likely to involve even closer integration with AI technologies. Combining IoT with AI enables predictive analytics, where systems can forecast potential quality issues based on patterns in sensor data. This AI-driven approach will enhance quality control by providing manufacturers with advanced insights that support more proactive and preventive quality strategies.

Edge Computing for Faster Decision-Making: Edge computing processes data near its source, such as directly on the production floor, rather than sending it to a centralized cloud server. This localized data processing reduces latency, allowing real-time decisions to be made faster. Edge computing will be particularly valuable in high-speed production environments where rapid response times are essential for maintaining quality.

More Specialized Sensors and Advanced Capabilities: The next generation of smart sensors will likely feature advanced capabilities, such as self-calibration, self-diagnosis, and multi-parameter sensing. These improvements will increase the reliability of sensors and expand the types of data they can collect. For instance, multi-parameter sensors could simultaneously monitor temperature, pressure, and humidity, providing more comprehensive data on environmental conditions affecting product quality.

Sustainable IoT Solutions: As sustainability becomes a priority, IoT and smart sensors are expected to support greener manufacturing practices. IoT can help companies track their environmental impact in real-time, optimizing resource usage, reducing waste, and enhancing energy efficiency. Smart sensors can also be designed with eco-friendly materials and low-power consumption to align with sustainability goals.

In conclusion, IoT and smart sensors are central to advancing quality management in the digital age. By enabling real-time monitoring, predictive maintenance, and data-driven optimization, they significantly enhance production efficiency, accuracy, and responsiveness. Despite challenges related to cost, security, and integration, the potential of IoT for transforming quality management practices is immense. As companies continue to adopt these technologies, they are better positioned to meet the demands of modern consumers and maintain high standards of product quality. The future of quality management, driven by IoT and sensor technology, promises to be more automated, accurate, and sustainable.

4.3 Big Data Analytics and Quality Control

In today's fast-paced manufacturing and service environments, the ability to leverage big data analytics for quality control has become a cornerstone for organizations seeking to improve their processes and products. The integration of big data analytics into quality control enables companies to derive meaningful insights from vast quantities of data, leading to enhanced decision-making, optimized quality processes, and ultimately, higher customer satisfaction. This section delves into how big data analytics can be utilized for root cause analysis and quality optimization, providing organizations with the tools necessary to maintain a competitive edge.

Understanding Big Data in Quality Control

Big data refers to the massive volumes of structured and unstructured data generated from various sources within an organization, such as production lines, customer feedback, supply chains, and market trends. This data is characterized by its volume, velocity, variety, and veracity—often referred to as the "four Vs" of big data. In the context of quality control, big data analytics encompasses the techniques and technologies used to analyze these large datasets to identify patterns, correlations, and anomalies that can impact product quality.

The shift towards a data-driven approach in quality control stems from the need for organizations to move beyond traditional methods that often rely on historical data and manual inspections. By harnessing the power of big data analytics, businesses can proactively address quality issues, enhance their understanding of customer preferences, and optimize processes for better overall performance.

1. Root Cause Analysis Through Big Data Analytics

Root cause analysis (RCA) is a systematic approach used to identify the underlying causes of defects or failures in products or processes. Traditional RCA methods often rely on anecdotal evidence or limited data, which can lead to incomplete or incorrect conclusions. However, big data analytics provides a more comprehensive framework for conducting RCA by aggregating and analyzing vast amounts of data from multiple sources.

A. Identifying Patterns and Trends

Big data analytics tools can sift through historical data from production processes, quality inspections, and customer feedback to identify patterns and trends that may not be immediately apparent. For instance, by analyzing defect rates in relation to various production parameters (such as machine settings, operator performance, and environmental conditions), organizations can uncover correlations that point to specific root causes of quality issues.

For example, if a particular machine consistently produces a higher rate of defects when operated at a certain temperature, this insight allows quality managers to investigate the machine's performance under those conditions. By focusing on these identified patterns, organizations can implement targeted improvements that address the root causes of defects rather than merely treating the symptoms.

B. Real-Time Monitoring and Alerting

One of the significant advantages of big data analytics is its ability to provide real-time monitoring of production processes. By implementing sensors and IoT devices that continuously collect data, organizations can analyze this information in real-time to detect anomalies and deviations from quality standards.

For instance, if a sensor detects that the pressure in a hydraulic press is fluctuating beyond acceptable limits, the analytics system can trigger an alert for immediate investigation. This proactive approach allows teams to address potential quality issues before they escalate into larger problems, reducing waste and enhancing overall product quality.

C. Utilizing Machine Learning for Predictive Analysis

Machine learning algorithms, a subset of big data analytics, can be employed to enhance root cause analysis by predicting potential quality issues before they occur. By training models on historical quality data, organizations can develop predictive analytics capabilities that forecast when and where defects are likely to arise.

For example, a manufacturer could use machine learning to analyze patterns of defects over time, considering variables such as machine wear, operator skill levels, and environmental factors. The model could then predict when a particular machine is likely to produce defects based on current operating conditions, allowing for preemptive maintenance or process adjustments. This capability not only reduces defect rates but also minimizes downtime and operational costs.

2. Quality Optimization Using Big Data Analytics

Quality optimization involves continuously improving processes to meet and exceed customer expectations while minimizing waste and costs. Big data analytics plays a critical role in quality optimization by providing actionable insights that drive continuous improvement initiatives.

A. Data-Driven Decision Making

Big data analytics empowers organizations to make data-driven decisions regarding quality improvement strategies. By analyzing data from various sources, including production metrics, customer feedback, and market trends, businesses can identify areas of improvement and implement targeted strategies to enhance quality.

For example, if data analysis reveals that customer complaints are highest for a specific product line, organizations can prioritize their improvement efforts in that area. This focus on data-driven decision-making ensures that resources are allocated effectively, maximizing the impact of quality initiatives.

B. Continuous Process Improvement (CPI)

Big data analytics enables organizations to adopt a continuous process improvement mindset. By establishing key performance indicators

(KPIs) and regularly analyzing data against these metrics, companies can identify trends and areas for improvement.

For instance, if a manufacturer tracks defect rates and notices an upward trend, data analytics can help identify the specific stages of the production process contributing to the increase. Armed with this information, quality teams can implement process changes, conduct training for operators, or optimize machine settings to address the identified issues.

C. Enhancing Customer Satisfaction

Ultimately, the goal of quality control is to enhance customer satisfaction. Big data analytics allows organizations to gain insights into customer preferences and expectations by analyzing feedback, reviews, and behavior patterns. This understanding can inform product development, quality standards, and service delivery.

For example, by analyzing customer feedback data, a company may discover that a particular feature is consistently praised while another is frequently criticized. This insight can drive product enhancements, leading to higher customer satisfaction and loyalty.

3. Challenges in Implementing Big Data Analytics for Quality Control

While the benefits of big data analytics in quality control are substantial, organizations must also navigate several challenges when implementing these systems.

Data Integration and Management: One of the primary challenges is integrating data from disparate sources. Organizations often have data silos across various departments, making it difficult to achieve a holistic view of quality metrics. Effective data management strategies and tools are necessary to unify data for analysis.

Skill Gap and Training: The successful implementation of big data analytics requires skilled personnel who understand both data analysis and quality control principles. Organizations may need to invest in training or hire data scientists to effectively leverage analytics for quality improvement.

Data Quality and Accuracy: The effectiveness of big data analytics hinges on the quality and accuracy of the data being analyzed. Organizations must establish robust data collection and validation processes to ensure that the insights derived from analytics are reliable and actionable.

Security and Compliance Concerns: With the increasing amount of data being collected, organizations must also consider data security and compliance with regulations such as GDPR or CCPA. Ensuring that customer and operational data is protected is paramount to maintaining trust and meeting legal requirements.

Big data analytics has revolutionized the field of quality control, providing organizations with the tools necessary to conduct thorough root cause analysis and optimize quality processes. By leveraging data-driven insights, companies can enhance their understanding of quality issues, implement targeted improvements, and ultimately deliver higher-quality products that meet customer expectations.

As organizations continue to embrace big data analytics, they will find that the ability to make informed decisions based on real-time data is essential for staying competitive in an increasingly complex marketplace. By addressing the challenges of implementation and fostering a culture of continuous improvement, businesses can harness the power of big data to transform their quality control practices and achieve lasting success.

4.4 Blockchain in Quality Assurance

In recent years, blockchain technology has emerged as a revolutionary tool that can significantly enhance quality assurance processes across various industries, particularly in supply chain management. By providing a decentralized, transparent, and secure method of recording and verifying transactions, blockchain offers unprecedented opportunities for improving the integrity and traceability of quality assurance measures. This section explores how blockchain technology can be leveraged to ensure transparency and traceability in supply chain quality management, along with its potential benefits, challenges, and real-world applications.

Understanding Blockchain Technology

At its core, blockchain is a distributed ledger technology that records transactions in a manner that is secure, transparent, and immutable. Each transaction is grouped into a block, which is then cryptographically linked to the previous block, forming a chain. This structure creates a permanent and tamper-resistant record of all transactions across a network.

Key characteristics of blockchain include:

Decentralization: Unlike traditional databases, which are controlled by a central authority, blockchain operates on a peer-to-peer network, allowing multiple participants to maintain their own copies of the ledger.

Transparency: All transactions recorded on the blockchain are visible to all network participants, enhancing accountability and trust.

Immutability: Once a transaction is recorded on the blockchain, it cannot be altered or deleted, ensuring the integrity of the data.

Security: Blockchain employs cryptographic techniques to secure data, making it resistant to unauthorized access and tampering.

These characteristics make blockchain particularly well-suited for quality assurance in supply chain management, where transparency and traceability are critical.

1. Enhancing Transparency in Supply Chain Quality Management

Transparency is a cornerstone of effective quality assurance, as it allows stakeholders to understand and trust the processes involved in producing and delivering products. Blockchain technology enhances transparency in several ways:

A. Real-Time Access to Information

By utilizing blockchain, all parties in the supply chain can access real-time information about products, including their origin, production processes, and handling. For example, if a manufacturer sources raw materials from multiple suppliers, the blockchain can provide a comprehensive view of the entire supply chain, including details about the conditions under which the materials were produced and processed.

This level of transparency empowers stakeholders, including manufacturers, suppliers, and consumers, to verify the quality of materials and products at every stage of the supply chain. For instance, a retailer can confidently communicate to customers that a product is sustainably sourced, as they can trace its origins back to certified suppliers on the blockchain.

B. Accountability and Trust

Blockchain's transparent nature fosters accountability among supply chain participants. Each transaction is recorded and timestamped, creating an audit trail that can be traced back to its source. This audit trail is crucial for identifying and addressing quality issues when they arise.

For example, if a batch of products is found to be defective, stakeholders can quickly trace back through the blockchain to identify where the problem originated, whether it was in the sourcing of raw materials, production, or distribution. This accountability encourages suppliers and manufacturers to adhere to high-quality standards, knowing that their actions are being recorded and monitored.

C. Reducing Fraud and Counterfeiting

In industries such as pharmaceuticals and luxury goods, counterfeiting and fraud can pose significant challenges to quality assurance. Blockchain's immutable records help combat these issues by ensuring that only verified products are sold to consumers.

For instance, pharmaceutical companies can use blockchain to track medications from the point of manufacture to the point of sale. This not only verifies the authenticity of the drugs but also provides consumers with the confidence that they are receiving genuine products. Additionally, it allows regulatory bodies to conduct audits more effectively, as they can easily access detailed records of the supply chain.

2. Ensuring Traceability in Quality Management

Traceability is the ability to track and trace the history of a product through its entire supply chain journey. This capability is essential for quality management, especially when dealing with recalls, compliance, and risk management. Blockchain technology enhances traceability in the following ways:

A. End-to-End Tracking

With blockchain, every step a product takes through the supply chain can be recorded, creating a complete history of the product from its origin to the end consumer. This end-to-end tracking is vital for industries where compliance with regulatory standards is mandatory.

For example, in the food industry, blockchain can be used to trace the journey of food products from farm to table. If a food safety issue arises, such as a contamination outbreak, regulators can quickly identify the source of the problem and implement necessary recalls. This not only protects consumers but also helps maintain the brand's reputation.

B. Facilitating Compliance and Audits

Regulatory compliance is critical for many industries, and maintaining comprehensive records is often a requirement. Blockchain simplifies compliance by providing a transparent and secure way to store documentation and records related to quality assurance.

For example, companies in the automotive industry must comply with strict safety and quality standards. By utilizing blockchain, manufacturers can easily provide regulators with access to a complete record of their quality control processes, including testing and inspections, without the need for cumbersome paperwork.

C. Rapid Response to Quality Issues

When quality issues arise, having a reliable traceability system in place is essential for minimizing risk and addressing the problem swiftly. Blockchain enables organizations to react quickly by providing immediate access to relevant data about the affected products.

For instance, if a batch of electronic components is found to be faulty, companies can utilize blockchain to pinpoint which specific components are affected and where they have been distributed. This rapid response capability is crucial for mitigating the impact of quality issues on customers and the organization.

3. Challenges and Considerations in Implementing Blockchain for Quality Assurance

While the benefits of blockchain in quality assurance are significant, organizations must also consider several challenges when implementing this technology:

Integration with Existing Systems: Integrating blockchain with existing supply chain management systems can be complex. Organizations may need to invest in new technology and processes to fully leverage blockchain's capabilities.

Stakeholder Collaboration: Successful implementation of blockchain requires collaboration among all stakeholders in the supply chain. This can be challenging, as different organizations may have varying levels of willingness to share data and adopt new technologies.

Data Privacy and Security Concerns: While blockchain is secure, organizations must still consider data privacy issues, particularly when dealing with sensitive information. Ensuring that confidential data is protected while still maintaining transparency is a critical consideration.

Regulatory Uncertainty: Blockchain technology is still relatively new, and regulatory frameworks are evolving. Organizations must stay informed about regulations that may impact their use of blockchain for quality assurance.

Blockchain technology holds immense potential for enhancing quality assurance in supply chain management. By providing transparency and traceability, blockchain can improve accountability, reduce fraud, and enable rapid responses to quality issues. As organizations increasingly embrace this technology, they can build more resilient and trustworthy supply chains that not only meet regulatory requirements but also exceed customer expectations.

While challenges remain in implementing blockchain solutions, the benefits of improved quality assurance processes make it a worthwhile investment for organizations looking to thrive in an increasingly competitive and complex market. As the technology matures and regulatory frameworks are established, blockchain is poised to become a cornerstone of quality management in the digital age.

5. Software and Digital Tools for Quality Management

As organizations continue to evolve in an increasingly digital landscape, the importance of leveraging technology for quality management has become paramount. Quality Management Software (QMS) has emerged as a critical tool that facilitates the implementation and monitoring of quality processes, ensuring compliance with standards, and enhancing overall product quality. This chapter explores the landscape of digital QMS, examining its features, benefits, and notable examples of software platforms available today.

5.1 Overview of Digital Quality Management Software (QMS)

Quality Management Software (QMS) refers to a suite of integrated tools designed to help organizations manage and improve quality across various processes. These tools are essential for businesses striving to achieve high levels of quality in their products and services, as they automate many quality management tasks, enhance visibility, and improve communication among team members.

A. Features of Digital QMS Platforms

Digital QMS platforms come equipped with a variety of features that cater to the needs of quality management within organizations. These features not only streamline processes but also provide actionable insights that drive continuous improvement. Some of the most common features include:

Document Control

One of the fundamental aspects of quality management is maintaining accurate and up-to-date documentation. Digital QMS systems allow organizations to create, store, and manage documents electronically. This feature ensures that employees always have access to the latest versions of quality manuals, standard operating procedures (SOPs), and other critical documents.

Document control features often include version control, which tracks changes made to documents and provides an audit trail, ensuring compliance with industry standards.

Audit Management

Digital QMS platforms typically include tools for planning, executing, and reporting on audits. This feature streamlines the auditing process, making it easier for organizations to identify non-conformities, assess compliance with regulations, and implement corrective actions.

Automated reminders and workflows can help ensure that audits are conducted on schedule, and results can be easily shared with relevant stakeholders.

CAPA (Corrective and Preventive Action) Management

A key component of any quality management system is the ability to identify, document, and resolve quality issues. Digital QMS platforms often include robust CAPA management tools that facilitate the entire process from identifying a problem to implementing corrective and preventive actions.

These tools help organizations track the root cause of issues, assess the effectiveness of actions taken, and close the loop by ensuring that problems are not repeated in the future.

Quality Reporting and Analytics

Digital QMS platforms typically feature reporting and analytics capabilities that enable organizations to visualize quality data and track performance metrics over time. Users can generate customizable reports that highlight trends, identify areas for improvement, and facilitate data-driven decision-making.

These insights are invaluable for senior management, as they provide a comprehensive overview of the organization's quality performance and facilitate strategic planning.

Training Management

Ensuring that employees are trained and competent in quality management practices is crucial for maintaining quality standards. Digital QMS platforms often include training management features that allow organizations to create, track, and manage training programs.

These tools can include e-learning modules, scheduling tools, and tracking of employee certifications, helping organizations ensure compliance and maintain a skilled workforce.

Supplier Quality Management

Managing supplier quality is essential for maintaining the overall quality of products and services. Many digital QMS platforms include features for evaluating and monitoring supplier performance, enabling organizations to ensure that suppliers meet quality standards.

This may involve tracking supplier audits, assessing quality metrics, and facilitating communication with suppliers regarding quality expectations and issues.

Risk Management

Identifying and managing risks associated with quality is an essential aspect of quality management. Digital QMS platforms often include risk management features that allow organizations to assess, prioritize, and mitigate risks related to quality.

These tools can help organizations implement proactive measures to minimize the likelihood of quality issues occurring, thereby enhancing overall product reliability.

Integration Capabilities

A significant advantage of digital QMS platforms is their ability to integrate with other software solutions used within the organization. Integration capabilities allow for seamless data sharing between systems, enhancing overall operational efficiency.

Common integrations include enterprise resource planning (ERP) systems, customer relationship management (CRM) systems, and manufacturing execution systems (MES), enabling organizations to have a holistic view of their operations.

B. Benefits of Digital QMS Platforms

The adoption of digital QMS platforms offers numerous benefits that can significantly enhance an organization's quality management efforts. Some of the key advantages include:

Improved Efficiency and Productivity

By automating routine quality management tasks, digital QMS platforms reduce the time and effort required to manage quality processes. This increased efficiency allows employees to focus on more value-added activities, ultimately enhancing overall productivity.

Enhanced Compliance

Many industries are subject to stringent regulatory requirements related to quality management. Digital QMS platforms help organizations maintain compliance by providing tools for document control, audit management, and training management. This ensures that organizations can easily demonstrate adherence to quality standards during audits and inspections.

Real-Time Visibility

Digital QMS platforms provide real-time visibility into quality metrics and processes, enabling organizations to monitor performance continuously. This visibility allows for quicker identification of quality issues and facilitates timely corrective actions, reducing the risk of non-conformities.

Data-Driven Decision Making

The reporting and analytics capabilities of digital QMS platforms enable organizations to make informed decisions based on accurate and up-to-date data. This data-driven approach supports continuous improvement initiatives and helps organizations align their quality management strategies with overall business goals.

Greater Collaboration and Communication

Digital QMS platforms foster collaboration and communication among team members by providing a centralized repository for quality-related information. This centralized approach ensures that all stakeholders have access to the information they need to perform their roles effectively, reducing the likelihood of miscommunication and errors.

Scalability

As organizations grow and evolve, their quality management needs may change. Digital QMS platforms are often designed to be scalable, allowing organizations to easily add new users, features, and functionalities as needed. This adaptability ensures that the QMS can grow alongside the organization.

Enhanced Customer Satisfaction

Ultimately, effective quality management leads to improved product quality and customer satisfaction. By implementing a digital QMS, organizations can ensure that they consistently meet customer expectations, leading to higher levels of customer loyalty and positive brand reputation.

C. Examples of Popular QMS Software

There are numerous digital QMS platforms available on the market, each offering unique features and functionalities tailored to different industries and organizational needs. Here are a few notable examples of popular QMS software:

MasterControl

MasterControl is a comprehensive quality management software solution designed for regulated industries such as pharmaceuticals, biotechnology, and medical devices. It offers a wide range of features, including document control, audit management, CAPA management, and training management. MasterControl's robust reporting and analytics capabilities help organizations track compliance and performance metrics effectively.

ETQ Reliance

ETQ Reliance is a cloud-based QMS platform that provides organizations with tools to manage quality processes across various industries. Its features include document control, incident management, audit management, and risk management. ETQ Reliance is known for its flexibility and scalability, making it suitable for organizations of all sizes.

Greenlight Guru

reenlight Guru is specifically designed for medical device companies, providing a complete QMS solution that aligns with regulatory requirements. Key features include document control, design control, risk management, and audit management. Greenlight Guru also offers integrations with other tools used in the product development lifecycle, enhancing collaboration among teams.

Sparta Systems' TrackWise

TrackWise is a leading quality management solution that offers comprehensive features for managing quality processes in regulated industries. Its capabilities include document management, CAPA management, and compliance management. TrackWise provides organizations with robust reporting tools and analytics to support data-driven decision-making.

IQMS

IQMS is an integrated ERP and QMS solution tailored for manufacturing organizations. Its quality management features include quality tracking, non-conformance management, and supplier quality management. IQMS helps organizations streamline their quality processes while also integrating with manufacturing operations for greater efficiency.

ISO 9001:2015 QMS Software

This is a specific category of QMS software designed to help organizations comply with the ISO 9001:2015 standard. These platforms typically provide features such as document control, audit management, and CAPA management tailored to meet the requirements of the ISO standard. Various providers offer ISO 9001-compliant software, allowing organizations to choose a solution that best fits their needs.

Qualio

Qualio is a cloud-based quality management software designed for life sciences companies. It provides tools for document management, training, and quality event management. Qualio is known for its user-friendly interface and emphasizes collaboration, enabling teams to work together effectively on quality initiatives.

Digital Quality Management Software (QMS) plays a pivotal role in modern organizations striving for excellence in quality management. With features that enhance efficiency, improve compliance, and provide real-time visibility into quality processes, digital QMS platforms empower organizations to achieve higher levels of quality and customer satisfaction.

As organizations continue to navigate the challenges of the digital age, leveraging the capabilities of digital QMS software will be essential for maintaining a competitive edge and fostering a culture of continuous improvement. By investing in the right QMS tools, organizations can transform their quality management practices and build a foundation for long-term success.

5.2 Statistical Process Control (SPC) and Automation Tools

In the realm of quality management, Statistical Process Control (SPC) plays a crucial role in ensuring that processes remain within predefined limits and deliver products that meet quality standards. With the advent of digital technologies, SPC has evolved, becoming more integrated and automated, enabling organizations to leverage real-time data for improved decision-making and quality outcomes. This section explores the role of SPC software in digital quality management and the impact of automation on data collection, analysis, and reporting.

A. Role of SPC Software in Digital Quality Management

Statistical Process Control (SPC) is a method used to monitor and control a process through the use of statistical methods. Its primary goal is to identify variations in the process and determine whether those variations are due to common causes (inherent to the process) or special causes (resulting from external factors). By employing SPC techniques, organizations can ensure that their processes are stable and capable of producing high-quality products consistently.

Real-Time Monitoring

One of the significant benefits of SPC software is its ability to monitor processes in real time. By collecting data directly from production lines or other operational areas, SPC software can analyze the data instantly to identify trends, deviations, and out-of-control conditions. This capability allows organizations to respond quickly to potential quality issues before they escalate, reducing waste and preventing defective products from reaching customers.

Control Charts

SPC software utilizes control charts to visualize process performance over time. Control charts help identify patterns and trends, making it easier to distinguish between common and special causes of variation. By plotting data points against control limits, organizations can determine whether a process is in control or requires corrective actions.

Various types of control charts exist, including X-bar charts, R charts, p-charts, and C-charts, each suited for different types of data. SPC software can automate the creation and updating of these charts, making it easier for quality professionals to interpret data and make informed decisions.

Root Cause Analysis

When variations are detected, SPC software can assist in performing root cause analysis to identify the underlying causes of the issue. By analyzing data trends, performing capability analysis, and utilizing tools like Pareto analysis and Fishbone diagrams, organizations can pinpoint the factors contributing to quality problems.

The insights gained from root cause analysis enable organizations to implement targeted corrective and preventive actions, ultimately improving process stability and product quality.

Integration with Other Quality Tools

Modern SPC software often integrates seamlessly with other quality management tools and systems, such as Quality Management Systems (QMS), Enterprise Resource Planning (ERP) systems, and Manufacturing Execution Systems (MES). This integration ensures that quality data is collected consistently and can be analyzed in conjunction with other operational data.

For example, integrating SPC software with an ERP system allows organizations to correlate quality data with production schedules, inventory levels, and supplier performance, providing a comprehensive view of quality across the organization.

Compliance and Reporting

Many industries have regulatory requirements regarding quality standards and reporting. SPC software simplifies compliance by providing automated reporting capabilities that generate documentation needed for audits and inspections. Organizations can produce reports on process performance, control charts, and quality metrics, demonstrating adherence to quality standards and regulations.

Automated reporting not only saves time but also reduces the risk of errors associated with manual data entry and reporting processes.

B. Automation in Data Collection, Analysis, and Reporting

The integration of automation into quality management processes has transformed how organizations collect, analyze, and report quality data. Automation tools enhance efficiency, accuracy, and responsiveness in quality management practices, leading to improved overall quality outcomes.

Automated Data Collection

Traditionally, data collection in quality management involved manual processes that were often time-consuming and prone to errors. With automation, organizations can utilize various data collection methods, such as sensors, IoT devices, and automated measurement systems, to capture quality-related data in real time.

Automated data collection ensures that organizations have access to accurate and timely information, enabling them to monitor processes continuously and identify potential quality issues before they impact production.

Data Analysis and Interpretation

Once data is collected, automated analysis tools can process vast amounts of information quickly and accurately. Advanced analytics algorithms can identify trends, correlations, and anomalies in the data that might not be immediately apparent through manual analysis.

Automation in data analysis allows quality professionals to focus on interpreting results and making strategic decisions rather than spending excessive time on data processing. This shift enhances the overall effectiveness of quality management efforts.

Real-Time Alerts and Notifications

Automated systems can be configured to trigger alerts and notifications when quality metrics fall outside predefined thresholds. These alerts can be sent to relevant personnel, such as quality managers or production supervisors, enabling them to take immediate action to address potential quality issues.

Real-time alerts facilitate proactive decision-making, allowing organizations to respond swiftly to deviations and maintain control over quality processes.

Predictive Analytics

Automation has paved the way for predictive analytics in quality management. By analyzing historical data and using machine learning algorithms, organizations can predict future quality issues before they occur. Predictive analytics can identify patterns that indicate an impending quality failure, enabling organizations to implement preventive measures proactively.

For instance, predictive models can forecast equipment failures based on historical performance data, allowing maintenance teams to address potential issues before they disrupt production.

Streamlined Reporting Processes

Automation simplifies the reporting process by generating reports automatically based on collected data and predefined criteria. Organizations can create customized dashboards that provide real-time insights into quality performance, allowing stakeholders to monitor key quality metrics effortlessly.

Automated reporting not only saves time but also enhances the accuracy of reports, ensuring that decision-makers have access to reliable information for strategic planning.

Enhanced Collaboration and Communication

Automation tools facilitate collaboration among team members by providing a centralized platform for quality-related information. Teams can access real-time data, share insights, and collaborate on quality improvement initiatives from anywhere, promoting a culture of continuous improvement.

By breaking down silos and enhancing communication, organizations can foster a more collaborative approach to quality management, leading to better outcomes.

Integration with Other Systems

Automation tools can integrate seamlessly with other enterprise systems, such as ERP, MES, and CRM platforms, allowing for a holistic view of quality across the organization. This integration enables organizations to correlate quality data with other operational metrics, enhancing the overall effectiveness of quality management efforts.

For example, integrating quality data with production scheduling can help organizations optimize manufacturing processes while maintaining quality standards.

The integration of Statistical Process Control (SPC) and automation tools has transformed quality management in the digital age. SPC software plays a pivotal role in monitoring and controlling processes, while automation enhances data collection, analysis, and reporting capabilities. Together, these tools empower organizations to achieve higher levels of quality, improve compliance, and foster a culture of continuous improvement.

As organizations continue to navigate the complexities of the digital landscape, embracing SPC software and automation tools will be essential for maintaining a competitive edge and delivering products that meet or exceed customer expectations. By leveraging the power of data and automation, organizations can enhance their quality management practices, drive operational excellence, and ultimately achieve their business objectives.

5.3 Integrating Quality Tools with ERP and Other Systems

In today's digital landscape, organizations rely heavily on various enterprise systems to manage operations, track performance, and ensure product quality. Among these systems, Enterprise Resource Planning (ERP) stands out as a comprehensive solution that integrates key business functions, including finance, supply chain, manufacturing, and quality management. Integrating quality tools with ERP and other enterprise systems is essential for organizations seeking to synchronize quality data, streamline processes, and enhance overall performance. This section explores the importance of integration, key benefits, challenges, and best practices for achieving seamless synchronization between quality tools and enterprise systems.

A. Importance of Integration

The integration of quality tools with ERP and other enterprise systems allows organizations to break down data silos, ensuring that quality information flows seamlessly across departments and functions. This synchronization is crucial for several reasons:

Holistic View of Operations

Integrating quality tools with ERP systems provides a holistic view of operations, enabling organizations to see how quality affects every aspect of their business. Quality data from various sources, such as manufacturing processes, customer feedback, and supplier performance, can be aggregated and analyzed in conjunction with financial and operational data. This comprehensive view supports better decision-making and more effective resource allocation.

Improved Collaboration

When quality tools are integrated with ERP systems, teams across the organization can collaborate more effectively. Quality professionals can access real-time data related to production, inventory, and customer orders, facilitating cross-functional teamwork. Improved collaboration fosters a culture of quality awareness and accountability throughout the organization.

Enhanced Decision-Making

Access to synchronized quality data empowers decision-makers with the insights needed to identify trends, assess risks, and implement corrective actions promptly. By leveraging data from ERP systems, organizations can make informed decisions that prioritize quality improvement and customer satisfaction.

Streamlined Processes

Integration reduces manual data entry and the risk of errors associated with disparate systems. When quality tools are linked to ERP systems, data can flow automatically between systems, streamlining processes and enhancing operational efficiency. This automation allows quality professionals to focus on analysis and improvement rather than administrative tasks.

Real-Time Monitoring and Reporting

With integrated quality tools, organizations can monitor quality metrics in real-time and generate comprehensive reports effortlessly. This capability enhances transparency, enabling stakeholders to track performance and compliance against predefined quality standards.

B. Key Benefits of Integration

Integrating quality tools with ERP and other systems offers numerous benefits that contribute to improved quality management practices:

Data Accuracy and Consistency

By synchronizing quality data with ERP systems, organizations can ensure data accuracy and consistency across various departments. This reliability is vital for making informed decisions and maintaining compliance with quality standards and regulations.

Faster Response Times

Integration enables organizations to respond more quickly to quality issues as they arise. When quality data is readily accessible within the ERP system, teams can identify and address problems promptly, minimizing the impact on production and customer satisfaction.

Enhanced Quality Control

Integrated systems allow for more robust quality control measures. For instance, organizations can implement automated quality checks during production, using data from both quality tools and ERP systems to trigger alerts when deviations occur. This proactive approach helps prevent defects and ensures that only products meeting quality standards reach customers.

Improved Supplier Quality Management

Synchronizing quality data with ERP systems can enhance supplier quality management efforts. Organizations can track supplier performance metrics, such as defect rates and delivery times, and use this information to make data-driven decisions about supplier relationships. By integrating quality assessments into the procurement process, organizations can select suppliers that align with their quality objectives.

Cost Savings

Streamlining processes and improving data accuracy through integration can lead to significant cost savings. By reducing waste associated with quality failures and minimizing the need for rework, organizations can improve their bottom line while enhancing customer satisfaction.

C. Challenges of Integration

While the benefits of integrating quality tools with ERP and other systems are substantial, organizations may encounter several challenges during the integration process:

Complexity of Systems

Integrating disparate systems can be complex, particularly if organizations use legacy systems or multiple vendors. Ensuring compatibility and functionality across systems requires careful planning and execution.

Data Management Issues

Data quality is paramount for successful integration. Organizations must address issues related to data accuracy, consistency, and completeness to avoid errors during synchronization. Implementing data governance practices can help mitigate these challenges.

Change Management

Integrating quality tools with ERP systems may require changes in workflows and processes. Organizations must effectively manage change to ensure that employees are trained and prepared for new systems and practices.

Resource Constraints

Integration projects often require significant time and resources, including financial investments in technology and personnel. Organizations must allocate sufficient resources to ensure successful integration.

D. Best Practices for Successful Integration

To achieve successful integration of quality tools with ERP and other enterprise systems, organizations can follow several best practices:

Define Clear Objectives

Before embarking on an integration project, organizations should define clear objectives and goals for what they hope to achieve. Identifying key performance indicators (KPIs) can help measure the success of the integration.

Conduct a Thorough Assessment

Organizations should conduct a thorough assessment of their existing systems and processes to identify areas for improvement. Understanding current workflows and data flows will inform the integration strategy.

Choose the Right Technology

Selecting the right technology solutions for integration is critical. Organizations should consider compatibility, scalability, and ease of use when evaluating potential tools and platforms.

Engage Stakeholders

Engaging key stakeholders from various departments throughout the integration process can facilitate buy-in and collaboration. Including representatives from quality management, production, IT, and finance can ensure that the integrated system meets the needs of all users.

Implement Change Management Strategies

Organizations should develop change management strategies to support employees during the integration process. Providing training, resources, and ongoing support will help employees adapt to new systems and workflows.

Monitor and Evaluate Performance

Once integration is complete, organizations should continuously monitor and evaluate the performance of the integrated systems. Regular assessments can identify areas for further improvement and ensure that the integrated tools continue to meet quality management objectives.

Integrating quality tools with ERP and other enterprise systems is essential for organizations seeking to enhance quality management practices in the digital age. By synchronizing quality data across systems, organizations can achieve a holistic view of operations, improve collaboration, and make data-driven decisions that prioritize quality improvement. While challenges may arise during the integration process, following best practices can help organizations navigate these complexities and unlock the numerous benefits of seamless integration. Ultimately, effective integration of quality tools will lead to improved operational efficiency, reduced costs, and enhanced customer satisfaction, driving organizational success in an increasingly competitive landscape.

6. Data-Driven Quality Decision-Making

In an era defined by rapid technological advancements and increasing market competition, data-driven decision-making has emerged as a fundamental aspect of effective quality management. Organizations that harness the power of data can enhance their quality management processes, leading to improved products, services, and customer satisfaction. This chapter explores the pivotal role of data in quality management, emphasizing the importance of data accuracy and timeliness in decision-making.

6.1 The Role of Data in Quality Management

Data is at the heart of quality management, influencing how organizations assess performance, identify issues, and implement improvements. The role of data in quality management can be understood through several key facets:

A. Data as a Foundation for Quality Management

Quantifying Quality Metrics

Data enables organizations to quantify quality metrics, such as defect rates, customer complaints, and compliance with quality standards. By collecting and analyzing relevant data, organizations can track performance over time and assess whether quality objectives are being met.

Facilitating Continuous Improvement

Continuous improvement is a core principle of quality management. Data-driven approaches, such as Six Sigma and Lean methodologies, rely on data analysis to identify areas for improvement, eliminate waste, and enhance processes. Organizations that prioritize data collection and analysis can foster a culture of continuous improvement.

Supporting Root Cause Analysis

Effective problem-solving in quality management often requires identifying the root causes of defects or quality issues. Data plays a crucial role in root cause analysis by providing insights into patterns and trends that may not be immediately apparent. Techniques such as Pareto analysis, fishbone diagrams, and statistical process control (SPC) rely on accurate data to uncover underlying problems.

Enhancing Compliance and Risk Management

Many industries are subject to strict regulations and quality standards. Data-driven quality management helps organizations ensure compliance by tracking performance against these standards. Additionally, data can be used to assess and mitigate risks, allowing organizations to take proactive measures to prevent quality failures.

B. Importance of Data Accuracy and Timeliness

While the role of data in quality management is critical, the accuracy and timeliness of that data are equally important. Poor-quality data can lead to misguided decisions, wasted resources, and diminished quality outcomes. The following points highlight the significance of data accuracy and timeliness in quality decision-making:

Data Accuracy: The Cornerstone of Effective Decision-Making

Accurate data is essential for informed decision-making. When data is flawed or incomplete, organizations risk making decisions based on misinformation. For example, if defect rates are inaccurately reported, management may underestimate the severity of quality issues, leading to insufficient corrective actions. Therefore, organizations must implement robust data validation processes to ensure accuracy at every stage of data collection and analysis.

Timeliness: The Key to Responsive Decision-Making

Timeliness refers to the speed at which data is collected, analyzed, and reported. In the fast-paced business environment, timely access to data is critical for effective decision-making. Delayed data can hinder an organization's ability to respond to quality issues promptly. For instance, if customer feedback is not analyzed quickly, organizations may miss opportunities to address concerns and improve satisfaction. Timely data allows organizations to make real-time decisions that can prevent quality problems from escalating.

The Intersection of Data Accuracy and Timeliness

Achieving a balance between data accuracy and timeliness is crucial for effective quality management. While organizations strive for quick access to data, they must also prioritize accuracy to avoid making hasty decisions based on unreliable information. Investing in automated data collection and analysis tools can help organizations enhance both accuracy and timeliness. Real-time monitoring systems and dashboards can provide instant access to quality metrics while ensuring data integrity.

C. Data Sources for Quality Management

Organizations can leverage various data sources to support quality decision-making. Some common sources include:

Internal Data

Internal data encompasses information generated within the organization, including production data, inspection reports, employee feedback, and quality control records. This data is often collected through quality management systems (QMS), manufacturing execution systems (MES), and enterprise resource planning (ERP) systems.

Customer Feedback

Customer feedback is a valuable source of data for assessing product quality and service performance. Organizations can gather feedback through surveys, reviews, complaint records, and social media interactions. Analyzing customer feedback helps organizations identify areas for improvement and gauge customer satisfaction.

Supplier Data

Quality management extends beyond the organization to include suppliers and partners. Organizations should track supplier performance metrics, such as defect rates and delivery reliability, to ensure that incoming materials meet quality standards. Data-driven supplier quality management allows organizations to address issues early in the supply chain.

Market Data

Market data, including industry benchmarks and competitor analysis, can provide valuable insights into quality performance. Organizations can compare their quality metrics with industry standards to identify gaps and opportunities for improvement.

D. Implementing Data-Driven Quality Decision-Making

To effectively implement data-driven quality decision-making, organizations should consider the following steps:

Establish Clear Quality Goals

Organizations should define clear quality goals aligned with their strategic objectives. These goals will guide data collection efforts and help prioritize the metrics that matter most to quality management.

Develop Robust Data Collection Processes

Organizations need to establish comprehensive data collection processes that ensure accuracy and consistency. This may involve standardizing data entry formats, implementing automated data collection tools, and training employees on proper data handling procedures.

Invest in Data Analysis Tools

To extract valuable insights from collected data, organizations should invest in data analysis tools and software. Statistical analysis software, data visualization tools, and business intelligence platforms can help organizations analyze trends, identify patterns, and support decision-making.

Promote a Data-Driven Culture

Fostering a data-driven culture within the organization is essential for successful implementation. Employees at all levels should be encouraged to embrace data-driven practices and leverage data in their daily decision-making processes. Training and ongoing education can help build data literacy across the organization.

Continuously Monitor and Improve

Data-driven quality decision-making is an ongoing process. Organizations should continuously monitor performance against quality goals and adjust strategies based on data insights. Regularly reviewing and refining data collection and analysis processes will enhance the organization's ability to make informed decisions.

Data-driven quality decision-making is vital for organizations striving for excellence in quality management. By recognizing the role of data in quality processes and understanding the importance of data accuracy and timeliness, organizations can make informed decisions that lead to improved products, services, and customer satisfaction. As businesses continue to navigate the complexities of the digital age, harnessing the power of data will remain a key differentiator in achieving and maintaining high-quality standards. Organizations that prioritize data-driven approaches will not only enhance their quality management practices but also position themselves for success in an increasingly competitive landscape.

6.2 Predictive and Prescriptive Analytics

In the realm of quality management, the advent of big data and advanced analytics has transformed traditional decision-making processes into more sophisticated, data-driven strategies. Predictive and prescriptive analytics play a critical role in enabling organizations to forecast potential quality issues and recommend proactive measures to mitigate them. This section explores the concepts of predictive and prescriptive analytics, their applications in quality management, and their impact on overall quality performance.

A. Understanding Predictive Analytics

1. Definition and Purpose

Predictive analytics involves using historical data, statistical algorithms, and machine learning techniques to identify the likelihood of future outcomes based on past patterns. In quality management, predictive analytics can be employed to anticipate potential quality issues, defects, or failures before they occur, allowing organizations to take proactive measures to maintain quality standards.

2. Key Components of Predictive Analytics

Data Collection: Predictive analytics relies heavily on the collection of relevant data, including historical quality performance metrics, production processes, customer feedback, and environmental factors. This data serves as the foundation for building predictive models.

Statistical Techniques: Various statistical methods, such as regression analysis, time series analysis, and classification techniques, are employed to analyze historical data and develop predictive models. These models help identify trends and correlations that can be used to forecast future quality outcomes.

Machine Learning: Machine learning algorithms enhance predictive analytics by enabling systems to learn from data and improve predictions over time. Techniques such as decision trees, neural networks, and ensemble methods are commonly used in quality management applications.

3. Applications of Predictive Analytics in Quality Management

Defect Prediction: One of the primary applications of predictive analytics in quality management is defect prediction. By analyzing historical defect data, organizations can develop models that identify factors contributing to defects, allowing them to predict when and where defects are likely to occur in the production process.

Failure Mode Analysis: Predictive analytics can be used to conduct failure mode and effects analysis (FMEA) by assessing the potential impact of different failure modes on product quality. This proactive approach helps organizations prioritize risk mitigation efforts and allocate resources effectively.

Supplier Quality Prediction: Organizations can apply predictive analytics to assess supplier quality by analyzing past performance data. By identifying patterns and trends in supplier quality, organizations can predict potential issues and take steps to improve supplier performance.

B. Understanding Prescriptive Analytics

1. Definition and Purpose

While predictive analytics focuses on forecasting future outcomes, prescriptive analytics goes a step further by recommending specific actions to optimize performance and mitigate risks. In quality management, prescriptive analytics helps organizations determine the best course of action to address predicted quality issues, ensuring that they achieve desired quality outcomes.

2. Key Components of Prescriptive Analytics

Optimization Algorithms: Prescriptive analytics utilizes optimization algorithms to evaluate various scenarios and recommend the best course of action based on defined objectives. These algorithms take into account constraints, trade-offs, and resource availability.

Simulation Modeling: Simulation techniques enable organizations to model different scenarios and assess the potential impact of various actions on quality outcomes. By simulating different approaches, organizations can identify the most effective strategies for quality improvement.

Decision Support Systems: Prescriptive analytics often incorporates decision support systems that provide decision-makers with actionable insights. These systems present recommendations based on predictive analytics results, historical data, and predefined business rules.

3. Applications of Prescriptive Analytics in Quality Management

Corrective Action Recommendations: After identifying potential quality issues through predictive analytics, prescriptive analytics can recommend specific corrective actions. For example, if a predictive model indicates a higher likelihood of defects in a particular production line, prescriptive analytics may suggest adjustments to processes, training for operators, or changes in materials used.

Resource Allocation: Prescriptive analytics can assist organizations in optimizing resource allocation to address quality issues. For instance, if a specific quality issue is predicted to arise, organizations can allocate additional resources, such as personnel or equipment, to the affected area to minimize the impact.

Continuous Improvement Strategies: Prescriptive analytics can guide organizations in developing continuous improvement strategies by recommending actions that align with overall quality objectives. By analyzing data from past improvement initiatives, organizations can identify successful strategies and replicate them in future efforts.

C. The Impact of Predictive and Prescriptive Analytics on Quality Management

The integration of predictive and prescriptive analytics into quality management processes offers several key benefits:

1. Proactive Quality Management

By leveraging predictive analytics, organizations can transition from reactive quality management—where issues are addressed only after they occur—to a proactive approach that anticipates and mitigates quality risks before they materialize. This shift not only improves overall quality but also reduces costs associated with rework, scrap, and customer dissatisfaction.

2. Enhanced Decision-Making

Predictive and prescriptive analytics provide decision-makers with data-driven insights that enhance the quality of decision-making. By understanding potential quality issues and receiving actionable recommendations, organizations can make informed choices that align with their quality objectives.

3. Increased Operational Efficiency

The ability to predict quality issues and prescribe corrective actions allows organizations to streamline their operations. By addressing potential problems before they escalate, organizations can minimize downtime, reduce waste, and enhance overall operational efficiency.

4. Improved Customer Satisfaction

Proactive quality management driven by predictive and prescriptive analytics leads to higher-quality products and services. As organizations consistently meet or exceed quality expectations, customer satisfaction improves, resulting in increased loyalty and repeat business.

D. Challenges and Considerations

While predictive and prescriptive analytics offer significant advantages, organizations must also be aware of potential challenges:

1. Data Quality and Availability

The effectiveness of predictive and prescriptive analytics relies heavily on the quality and availability of data. Organizations must ensure that data is accurate, complete, and relevant to achieve reliable predictions and actionable recommendations.

2. Complexity of Implementation

Implementing predictive and prescriptive analytics can be complex, requiring specialized skills and technology. Organizations may need to invest in training and resources to develop and maintain effective analytics capabilities.

3. Resistance to Change

Cultural resistance to change can hinder the adoption of data-driven approaches. Organizations must foster a culture that embraces data-driven decision-making and encourages collaboration across departments to successfully implement predictive and prescriptive analytics.

Predictive and prescriptive analytics represent a transformative shift in quality management, enabling organizations to anticipate quality issues and recommend effective corrective actions. By leveraging these advanced analytics techniques, organizations can enhance their quality management processes, achieve higher quality standards, and drive continuous improvement. As the business landscape becomes increasingly data-driven, the integration of predictive and prescriptive analytics will be essential for organizations seeking to remain competitive and responsive to changing market demands.

6.3 Building a Data-Driven Quality Culture

In today's rapidly evolving business environment, organizations that leverage data effectively are positioned to achieve superior quality outcomes. Building a data-driven quality culture is essential for companies striving to enhance their quality management processes. This chapter will explore the critical components of fostering a data-driven mindset within organizations and the importance of training and development for data literacy among quality teams.

A. Understanding a Data-Driven Quality Culture

A data-driven quality culture refers to an organizational ethos that prioritizes the use of data and analytics in decision-making, problem-solving, and continuous improvement processes. In this culture, data is not merely seen as a collection of numbers but as a valuable asset that drives insights, informs strategies, and shapes the organization's approach to quality management.

1. Characteristics of a Data-Driven Quality Culture

A data-driven quality culture possesses several defining characteristics:

Data as a Core Value: Organizations in this culture place high value on data and see it as integral to achieving quality objectives. Leadership promotes data usage at all levels of the organization.

Transparency and Openness: Information sharing is encouraged, leading to a transparent environment where team members can access relevant data and insights.

Collaborative Decision-Making: Data-driven cultures promote collaboration across departments, allowing diverse perspectives to inform quality decisions.

Continuous Improvement: Organizations embrace a mindset of learning and improvement, using data to identify areas for enhancement and implement solutions.

Empowerment: Employees are empowered to utilize data in their roles, enabling them to take ownership of quality initiatives.

B. Encouraging a Data-Driven Mindset within the Organization

Fostering a data-driven mindset requires a systematic approach that involves leadership commitment, clear communication, and the development of data-friendly policies and practices.

1. Leadership Commitment

The commitment of organizational leaders is crucial for building a data-driven quality culture. Leaders set the tone for the organization, and their support can inspire employees to adopt data-driven practices.

Vision and Strategy: Leaders must articulate a clear vision for how data will be used to enhance quality management. This vision should align with the organization's overall strategy and objectives.

Role Modeling: Leaders should demonstrate data-driven decision-making in their actions. By using data to inform their choices, they model the behavior they expect from employees.

Resource Allocation: Investing in the necessary tools, technologies, and training programs is essential for supporting data-driven initiatives. Leaders should prioritize resources that enable data collection, analysis, and reporting.

2. Communication and Engagement

Effective communication is vital for promoting a data-driven mindset across the organization. Employees should understand the importance of data and how it contributes to quality management.

Storytelling with Data: Leaders can use storytelling techniques to illustrate the impact of data on quality outcomes. Sharing success stories and case studies can help employees see the value of data-driven practices.

Regular Updates: Providing regular updates on quality initiatives, data usage, and results helps keep employees engaged and informed. This transparency fosters a sense of ownership and encourages participation in data-driven initiatives.

3. Creating Data-Driven Policies and Practices

To embed a data-driven mindset within the organization, it is essential to establish policies and practices that prioritize data usage.

Data Governance: Implementing data governance frameworks ensures that data is accurate, reliable, and accessible. Clear guidelines for data collection, storage, and usage foster a culture of accountability.

Data Accessibility: Organizations should prioritize making data easily accessible to employees. This can involve implementing user-friendly data visualization tools and dashboards that allow team members to interact with data and derive insights.

Recognition and Rewards: Recognizing and rewarding employees who demonstrate data-driven behaviors can reinforce the importance of a data-driven mindset. This can include formal recognition programs or informal acknowledgment during team meetings.

C. Training and Development for Data Literacy in Quality Teams

While promoting a data-driven mindset is essential, organizations must also invest in training and development to ensure that employees possess the necessary data literacy skills to effectively utilize data in their roles.

1. Importance of Data Literacy

Data literacy refers to the ability to read, understand, create, and communicate data. In the context of quality management, data literacy is critical for enabling employees to make informed decisions based on data insights.

Empowerment through Data Literacy: Employees with data literacy skills feel more empowered to utilize data in their work. They can analyze trends, identify patterns, and make evidence-based decisions, leading to improved quality outcomes.

Enhanced Collaboration: Data literacy fosters collaboration among team members as they share insights, challenge assumptions, and work together to solve quality issues. A common understanding of data terminology and concepts enables effective communication.

2. Assessing Data Literacy Needs

Organizations should assess the data literacy needs of their quality teams to develop targeted training programs.

Skill Assessment: Conducting skill assessments can help identify gaps in data literacy among employees. This can involve surveys, interviews, or assessments that evaluate employees' data-related skills and knowledge.

Role-Specific Training: Different roles within quality management may require different levels of data literacy. Tailoring training programs to meet the specific needs of various roles ensures that employees acquire relevant skills.

3. Designing Data Literacy Training Programs

Once the training needs are assessed, organizations can design data literacy training programs that align with their goals.

Foundational Training: Offering foundational training on data concepts, terminology, and basic analytics skills is essential for building a common understanding among employees. This can include workshops, online courses, or in-person training sessions.

Advanced Analytics Training: For employees involved in data analysis and interpretation, advanced training on statistical methods, data visualization techniques, and analytical tools is crucial. This training enables them to derive meaningful insights from data.

Hands-On Learning Opportunities: Providing hands-on learning opportunities, such as real-world projects or simulations, allows employees to apply their data literacy skills in practical contexts. This experiential learning enhances retention and understanding.

4. Encouraging Continuous Learning

Building a data-driven culture requires ongoing commitment to data literacy and continuous learning.

Access to Resources: Organizations should provide access to resources, such as online courses, webinars, and industry publications, that support ongoing learning in data literacy and analytics.

Peer Learning and Collaboration: Encouraging peer learning and collaboration can foster a culture of knowledge-sharing. Employees can participate in study groups, workshops, or knowledge-sharing sessions to enhance their data literacy skills together.

Feedback and Improvement: Organizations should solicit feedback on training programs to identify areas for improvement. Regular evaluations can help ensure that training remains relevant and effective.

D. Measuring Success and Impact

To gauge the effectiveness of efforts to build a data-driven quality culture, organizations should implement measures to track progress.

1. Key Performance Indicators (KPIs)

Establishing KPIs related to data usage and quality outcomes can provide valuable insights into the impact of a data-driven culture.

Data Utilization Metrics: Tracking metrics related to data utilization, such as the frequency of data access, usage of analytics tools, and participation in data-related training programs, can provide insights into the adoption of data-driven practices.

Quality Performance Metrics: Monitoring quality performance metrics, such as defect rates, customer satisfaction scores, and process improvement outcomes, can help organizations assess the effectiveness of data-driven initiatives.

2. Continuous Improvement Feedback Loops

Implementing feedback loops allows organizations to gather insights from employees regarding the effectiveness of data-driven initiatives and training programs.

Surveys and Feedback Forms: Conducting regular surveys or feedback forms can provide valuable insights into employees' perceptions of data-driven practices and the effectiveness of training programs.

Focus Groups and Discussions: Organizing focus groups or discussions among quality teams can facilitate open dialogue about challenges, successes, and areas for improvement. This collaborative approach fosters a sense of ownership and engagement.

E. Challenges in Building a Data-Driven Quality Culture

While building a data-driven quality culture offers significant benefits, organizations may face challenges along the way.

1. Resistance to Change

Cultural resistance to change can impede efforts to establish a data-driven mindset. Employees may be accustomed to traditional decision-making approaches and may be hesitant to embrace data-driven practices.

Addressing Concerns: Organizations should actively address concerns and misconceptions about data usage. Providing clear explanations of the benefits of data-driven practices can help alleviate resistance.

2. Skills Gap

The skills gap in data literacy can pose challenges for organizations. Employees may lack the necessary skills to effectively interpret and utilize data, hindering their ability to engage in data-driven quality management.

Investing in Training: Organizations must prioritize training and development to bridge the skills gap. This investment is essential for enabling employees to leverage data effectively.

3. Resource Limitations

Limited resources, including time, budget, and technology, can hinder efforts to build a data-driven quality culture. Organizations may struggle to allocate the necessary resources for training and technology investments.

Strategic Prioritization: Organizations should prioritize initiatives that align with their quality goals. Focusing on high-impact areas can maximize the effectiveness of resource allocation.

Building a data-driven quality culture is essential for organizations aiming to achieve superior quality management outcomes. By fostering a data-driven mindset, providing training and development for data literacy, and measuring success through relevant KPIs, organizations can create an environment where data is leveraged as a valuable asset. While challenges may arise, the benefits of a data-driven culture—proactive quality management, enhanced decision-making, and continuous improvement—far outweigh the obstacles. Embracing data-driven practices will empower organizations to thrive in today's competitive landscape, driving excellence in quality management and delivering value to customers.

7. Quality in Digital Supply Chains

7.1 Enhancing Quality across the Digital Supply Chain

In today's global and interconnected markets, digital supply chains are crucial for maintaining product quality, minimizing risks, and improving efficiency. Digital solutions enable supply chain managers to monitor quality in real-time, from procurement to delivery, and address issues proactively. This section examines digital solutions for quality assurance, especially in procurement and supplier management, to enhance end-to-end quality in the digital supply chain.

A. Importance of Quality in Digital Supply Chains

In digital supply chains, data flows seamlessly between suppliers, manufacturers, and customers, allowing organizations to maintain high standards. Quality assurance across the supply chain can reduce product recalls, avoid waste, and enhance customer satisfaction. With digital technologies, companies can now:

Monitor Product Quality at Every Stage: Quality control processes are embedded throughout the supply chain, ensuring that defects or issues are identified and resolved early.

Predict and Prevent Quality Issues: Analytics and AI-powered solutions can predict potential quality issues, allowing companies to mitigate risks proactively.

Ensure Compliance with Standards: Digital tools streamline compliance management, ensuring suppliers and partners adhere to industry regulations and standards.

B. Digital Solutions for Quality Assurance in Procurement

Procurement is a foundational aspect of supply chain management where quality begins. Digital tools play a crucial role in supplier selection, evaluation, and monitoring to ensure high standards from the onset.

1. Supplier Qualification and Evaluation Tools

Digital supplier management tools assess potential suppliers before onboarding them into the supply chain network. They enable businesses to evaluate factors such as:

Supplier History and Reputation: Digital platforms provide insights into a supplier's historical performance, compliance records, and previous partnerships.

Quality Certifications: By automating verification of quality certifications (such as ISO standards), companies ensure that suppliers meet required standards.

Risk Assessment Models: Risk assessment tools use data to analyze various risk factors, including financial stability, geopolitical risks, and past quality issues, which could impact quality outcomes.

2. Automated Procurement Processes

Automating procurement processes streamlines purchasing decisions and ensures quality by minimizing manual intervention and standardizing the workflow.

Automated Supplier Approval: Digital systems can automatically approve suppliers based on pre-defined quality criteria, which speeds up procurement while ensuring quality standards.

Contract Management: Digital platforms enable organizations to create contracts that specify quality standards, delivery timelines, and compliance requirements, and monitor adherence in real time.

3. Supplier Performance Management Platforms

Supplier performance management (SPM) platforms collect and analyze data on supplier performance over time, providing a comprehensive view of quality standards across the supply chain.

Real-Time Performance Metrics: Key metrics such as defect rates, on-time delivery, and customer complaints are tracked in real-time to ensure that suppliers consistently meet quality standards.

Corrective Action Tracking: SPM platforms enable companies to initiate corrective actions for suppliers if they fail to meet quality benchmarks. The platform provides an audit trail, documenting the issue and the corrective measures taken.

C. Quality Assurance through IoT and Smart Sensors

Internet of Things (IoT) devices and smart sensors are valuable in digital supply chains, particularly for real-time monitoring of goods, equipment, and environmental conditions.

1. Real-Time Quality Monitoring

Sensors placed on goods or in storage facilities monitor key quality parameters, such as temperature, humidity, and pressure, especially for perishable or sensitive products.

Cold Chain Management: In the food, pharmaceutical, and healthcare industries, maintaining a specific temperature is essential. IoT sensors continuously monitor temperature conditions and alert managers to deviations, ensuring compliance with quality standards.

Condition-Based Monitoring: Sensors detect vibrations, temperature fluctuations, or other conditions in real-time, alerting teams if there is a deviation that could impact product quality.

2. Digital Twin Technology

Digital twin technology creates a virtual model of a physical product or process, enabling companies to monitor performance, predict issues, and improve quality control.

Simulation and Testing: Companies can use digital twins to simulate various production and operational scenarios, allowing them to identify potential quality issues without impacting the actual supply chain.

Predictive Maintenance: Digital twins help forecast maintenance needs by simulating equipment wear and tear, reducing unplanned downtime and ensuring production quality.

D. Quality Assurance in Supplier Management

Managing suppliers effectively is crucial to maintaining quality standards across a global supply chain. Digital tools facilitate this by enhancing transparency, communication, and accountability with suppliers.

1. Supplier Collaboration Platforms

Supplier collaboration platforms enable real-time communication and data sharing between suppliers and the organization. These platforms provide suppliers with:

Access to Quality Standards: Suppliers have real-time access to the buyer's quality standards, specifications, and requirements, reducing misunderstandings.

Collaboration on Corrective Actions: When quality issues arise, supplier collaboration platforms allow suppliers and buyers to collaborate on corrective actions and track progress in real-time.

2. Supplier Scorecards and Dashboards

Digital scorecards and dashboards allow companies to evaluate supplier performance in terms of quality, delivery, cost, and responsiveness.

Customized Performance Indicators: Organizations can customize scorecards to include specific quality indicators, helping them track supplier adherence to quality standards.

Automated Alerts for Poor Performance: Scorecard systems often come with automated alerts that notify supply chain managers when a supplier falls below quality expectations.

3. Supplier Auditing and Compliance Monitoring

Regular auditing of suppliers is essential for maintaining quality standards. Digital solutions streamline the audit process and ensure ongoing compliance with quality requirements.

Remote Audits with IoT Data: IoT-enabled monitoring allows organizations to conduct remote audits by collecting data directly from the supplier's production facility.

Digital Audit Trail: Quality management platforms create a digital trail for all supplier audits, ensuring that organizations have a clear record of compliance and quality adherence.

E. Leveraging Advanced Analytics for Quality Insights

Data analytics plays an increasingly critical role in enhancing quality across digital supply chains. Advanced analytics tools help companies gain deeper insights into quality metrics, root causes of quality issues, and predictive insights for proactive quality management.

1. Root Cause Analysis and Continuous Improvement

Analytics software identifies root causes of quality problems by analyzing data from multiple sources across the supply chain. For example:

Defect Analysis: Advanced analytics software can identify patterns in defect occurrences, helping managers pinpoint whether the root cause is linked to raw materials, production processes, or supplier inconsistencies.

Continuous Improvement Initiatives: Data-driven insights enable organizations to implement continuous improvement initiatives, such as Six Sigma, to address quality issues proactively.

2. Predictive Quality Management

Predictive analytics uses historical data to forecast potential quality issues, allowing organizations to address problems before they occur.

Early Warning Systems: Predictive models identify risk factors associated with quality defects and alert managers when specific parameters are trending unfavorably.

Proactive Quality Adjustments: By analyzing data trends, organizations can make adjustments to production or sourcing processes to maintain quality standards, thus reducing waste and rework.

F. Benefits of Digital Solutions for Quality Assurance in Supply Chains

Digital solutions bring numerous benefits to quality assurance processes in the supply chain:

Enhanced Visibility: Real-time tracking of quality parameters and supplier performance improves transparency across the supply chain.

Improved Responsiveness: Automated alerts and predictive analytics enable quick responses to quality issues, reducing the likelihood of defective products reaching customers.

Cost Savings: By minimizing quality-related disruptions, digital solutions reduce the costs associated with rework, recalls, and waste.

Sustainability and Compliance: Digital tools ensure adherence to environmental standards and compliance regulations, which is critical for corporate social responsibility and brand reputation.

G. Challenges in Implementing Digital Quality Assurance in Supply Chains

While digital solutions offer numerous advantages, there are challenges to implementing digital quality assurance in supply chains:

Integration with Legacy Systems: Many companies still rely on legacy systems, making integration with advanced digital tools difficult.

Data Privacy and Security: As supply chains become more digital, ensuring data security and compliance with data privacy regulations (such as GDPR) becomes more complex.

Change Management: Employees and suppliers must adapt to new technologies and processes, which requires training and a shift in mindset.

High Initial Costs: Implementing digital quality assurance tools can involve significant upfront costs, particularly for smaller organizations.

Enhancing quality across digital supply chains is critical to maintaining high standards, minimizing risks, and meeting customer expectations.

By leveraging digital tools, organizations can monitor quality at every stage, from procurement to delivery, ensuring consistency and transparency. Through IoT sensors, supplier management platforms, and advanced analytics, companies can detect potential quality issues early, address root causes, and foster continuous improvement across their operations. While challenges such as data security and integration remain, the benefits of digital quality assurance solutions significantly outweigh these obstacles, positioning organizations to excel in today's competitive marketplace. As supply chains continue to evolve, embracing digital solutions for quality management will be essential for companies aiming to achieve operational excellence and deliver superior customer experiences.

7.2 Leveraging Blockchain for Transparency

Introduction to Blockchain in Quality Management

Blockchain technology has become a transformative force in various industries, offering unique advantages for enhancing transparency, traceability, and security across the supply chain. Originally designed for cryptocurrency, blockchain's inherent properties make it ideal for managing quality in complex supply chains by enabling immutable, transparent records of every transaction or quality check.

For quality management, blockchain can revolutionize transparency, allowing stakeholders to access secure, real-time data on product quality, provenance, and process compliance. This section explores the application of blockchain for transparency in quality management, examining real-world case studies that showcase its transformative potential.

A. Understanding Blockchain in Supply Chain Quality Management

Blockchain is essentially a decentralized ledger system that records transactions in a transparent, immutable way. Each "block" represents a transaction or a quality check in this case, linked to previous blocks, creating a "chain" that cannot be altered retroactively. This structure enhances trust and traceability, ensuring each stage of production and distribution meets established quality standards.

Key Benefits of Blockchain for Quality Management

Enhanced Transparency: Blockchain provides a transparent record accessible to all stakeholders. From raw materials to final product delivery, each step is visible and verifiable, reducing opportunities for fraud or error.

Traceability: Blockchain allows companies to trace every component and process back to its origin, which is crucial for industries where quality and safety are paramount, such as pharmaceuticals and food.

Data Integrity and Security: Data recorded on a blockchain cannot be altered or deleted, which ensures the accuracy of quality records. This immutability secures data against tampering and enhances accountability.

Real-Time Monitoring: Blockchain enables real-time monitoring of quality metrics, allowing organizations to react promptly to potential issues. This is particularly useful in industries with stringent regulatory standards.

Regulatory Compliance: Blockchain can simplify regulatory compliance by maintaining transparent, easily auditable records of quality and safety measures. It aids organizations in meeting various standards, including ISO, FDA, and HACCP guidelines.

B. Blockchain Use Cases in Quality Management

To illustrate the impact of blockchain on quality management, several industries have successfully implemented blockchain for quality assurance and transparency.

1. Food and Beverage Industry: Ensuring Product Safety

The food and beverage industry faces challenges in ensuring product quality and safety, as supply chains are often complex and involve multiple suppliers. Blockchain provides a powerful solution to address these challenges.

Case Study: Walmart and IBM's Food Trust Blockchain

Walmart, in collaboration with IBM, launched the Food Trust blockchain to improve traceability and food safety across its supply chain. The blockchain-based system enables Walmart to trace food products from farm to shelf within seconds, rather than days.

Process: Each step of the supply chain, from farmers to distributors to retailers, logs data into the blockchain. Details such as origin, handling conditions, and transport history are recorded in real-time.

Quality Control: This visibility allows Walmart to ensure suppliers adhere to strict quality standards and handle products safely. In case of contamination, Walmart can pinpoint the source immediately, minimizing potential health risks to consumers.

Results: The blockchain has reduced food recalls, improved quality control, and enhanced consumer trust, as customers know that Walmart can trace product origins and quality conditions at every stage.

2. Pharmaceutical Industry: Ensuring Authenticity and Compliance

In the pharmaceutical industry, counterfeit products are a significant issue that compromises patient safety. Blockchain enables pharmaceutical companies to verify the authenticity and quality of products at every stage of the supply chain.

Case Study: MediLedger Project

The MediLedger Project, initiated by companies like Pfizer and Genentech, uses blockchain to secure the pharmaceutical supply chain and combat counterfeit drugs.

Process: MediLedger records each transaction in the pharmaceutical supply chain on a decentralized ledger, capturing details about product provenance, quality control checks, and regulatory compliance.

Authentication and Compliance: By linking each product batch with a unique identifier on the blockchain, MediLedger provides a verifiable record of the product's journey, ensuring compliance with Good Manufacturing Practices (GMP) and other standards.

Results: MediLedger has improved traceability, reduced counterfeiting, and strengthened regulatory compliance. The project demonstrates how blockchain can create a tamper-proof record, ensuring product quality and patient safety.

3. Automotive Industry: Quality Control in Manufacturing

The automotive industry has complex manufacturing processes with thousands of components sourced from various suppliers. Ensuring each part meets quality standards is essential for safety and performance.

Case Study: BMW's PartChain Initiative

BMW's PartChain project uses blockchain to enhance transparency and traceability of automotive components. The project provides an immutable record of each part's history, ensuring suppliers meet BMW's stringent quality standards.

Process: Blockchain records the origin, manufacturing process, and quality control checks of each component. If a defect is identified, BMW can quickly trace the issue to the source, addressing it without disrupting the entire supply chain.

Quality Assurance: PartChain allows BMW to verify that each part meets design and safety requirements, supporting proactive quality control and minimizing the risk of recalls.

Results: BMW's blockchain initiative has enhanced supply chain transparency, streamlined quality assurance, and reduced defect rates, setting a new standard for quality management in the automotive industry.

4. Electronics Industry: Transparent Quality Tracking

The electronics industry relies on global supply chains and faces challenges in verifying the quality of components, especially for high-value and sensitive electronics.

Case Study: Foxconn and TSMC's Blockchain for Quality Assurance

Foxconn and TSMC, major players in electronics manufacturing, utilize blockchain to track the quality and provenance of components used in smartphones, computers, and other devices.

Process: Each component is tagged with a unique identifier, allowing it to be tracked through every production stage. Suppliers and manufacturers log quality checks, testing results, and certification data into a shared blockchain.

Quality Monitoring: If any defects arise, companies can quickly identify affected batches and trace issues to specific suppliers, minimizing disruption.

Results: This use of blockchain has improved traceability, reduced defect rates, and enhanced customer trust, as companies can guarantee the quality and origin of every component in their products.

5. Textile and Apparel Industry: Sustainability and Quality Tracking

Consumers increasingly demand transparency regarding product quality and sustainability in the textile industry. Blockchain can track materials from origin to end-user, ensuring sustainable and high-quality products.

Case Study: Provenance and Circular Fashion

Provenance, a blockchain company, partners with fashion brands to provide transparency in the supply chain, tracking the origin of materials and quality checks throughout production.

Process: Brands log details of each stage in the production process, from raw material sourcing to final product quality checks. Consumers can access this data via a digital product passport, ensuring transparency.

Sustainability and Quality: Blockchain confirms the ethical sourcing of materials and adherence to quality standards, allowing brands to meet both quality and environmental expectations.

Results: Provenance has helped fashion brands increase consumer trust and establish a reputation for sustainability and quality assurance, improving customer loyalty.

C. Challenges in Blockchain Implementation for Quality Management

While blockchain offers numerous benefits, it also presents challenges that organizations must consider:

Integration with Existing Systems: Integrating blockchain with traditional quality management systems can be complex, especially for organizations with legacy systems.

Data Privacy and Security: Blockchain records are immutable, raising concerns over data privacy, especially in regions with strict data protection laws like GDPR.

Cost and Scalability: Implementing blockchain can require significant investment, making it challenging for smaller companies or those with limited budgets.

Standardization Issues: Without industry-wide standards for blockchain, interoperability and data sharing across different platforms can be difficult.

Conclusion

Blockchain technology has proven to be a game-changer for transparency in quality management across industries. By creating a secure, transparent, and immutable record, blockchain enables companies to track product quality from origin to delivery, ensuring compliance and consumer trust. From Walmart's food traceability system to BMW's PartChain, these case studies illustrate the transformative potential of blockchain for enhancing transparency, accountability, and efficiency in quality management.

The successful implementation of blockchain requires companies to address integration, cost, and standardization challenges. However, as blockchain technology continues to mature and industry standards develop, it will play an increasingly crucial role in digital quality management, helping companies meet customer expectations for transparency, quality, and sustainability in an ever-evolving global market.

7.3 Quality Collaboration with Supply Chain Partners

In today's interconnected supply chains, quality management is no longer confined within a single organization but is a collaborative effort that involves suppliers, distributors, and other key partners. Effective quality collaboration ensures that all partners align with shared quality standards, contribute to continuous improvement, and meet end-customer expectations. Digital transformation has enabled a new level of collaboration by facilitating real-time data sharing, enhancing communication, and fostering transparency throughout the supply chain.

This section delves into best practices for establishing digital quality partnerships, focusing on the tools and approaches that can enhance quality collaboration among supply chain partners.

A. The Importance of Quality Collaboration in Supply Chains

Quality collaboration with supply chain partners is essential for several reasons:

Shared Quality Standards: Ensuring that all suppliers and partners adhere to uniform quality standards helps maintain product integrity and customer satisfaction. This is especially important in industries such as pharmaceuticals, electronics, and automotive, where defects can lead to significant safety risks and reputational damage.

Cost and Risk Reduction: Collaborative quality management reduces costs by minimizing rework, returns, and recalls. It also reduces risks by identifying and addressing quality issues early in the supply chain, preventing costly disruptions downstream.

Agility and Responsiveness: A collaborative approach allows partners to respond swiftly to quality issues, adapting to market changes and regulatory requirements with agility. Real-time data sharing facilitates faster decision-making and problem-solving, helping partners address quality concerns promptly.

Continuous Improvement: A collaborative environment fosters knowledge sharing and collective learning, which are critical for continuous improvement. Partners can share insights, best practices, and lessons learned, helping all stakeholders enhance their quality management processes.

Compliance and Regulatory Adherence: Many industries have stringent regulatory requirements for quality. Collaborating with supply chain partners ensures that all involved parties meet compliance standards, avoiding legal complications and penalties.

B. Best Practices for Digital Quality Partnerships

Digital transformation has empowered companies to build stronger quality collaborations by enabling transparent communication, real-time monitoring, and data sharing. Here are some best practices for establishing and maintaining effective digital quality partnerships:

1. Implementing Real-Time Data Sharing

Real-time data sharing is the cornerstone of digital quality collaboration. By exchanging data with supply chain partners, companies can maintain up-to-date records of quality metrics, track the origin and status of materials, and address issues as they arise.

Use of Cloud-Based Platforms: Cloud platforms enable real-time data sharing, allowing all partners to access quality metrics and audit trails. These platforms facilitate centralized data storage, making it easier for partners to share, view, and analyze information.

Data Standardization: For effective data sharing, companies should standardize data formats and quality metrics. This ensures that all parties can understand and use the information effectively, regardless of their systems.

Automated Alerts and Notifications: Automated alerts can notify partners of any quality deviations, helping them take corrective action immediately. This ensures timely intervention and reduces the risk of defects or compliance issues.

2. Using Collaborative Quality Management Software

Quality management software (QMS) with collaborative features enables companies to work more closely with their supply chain partners on quality initiatives. These platforms allow for centralized monitoring, shared documentation, and collaborative problem-solving.

Shared Quality Audits: Collaborative QMS allows partners to conduct joint audits and assessments. By reviewing quality processes together, they can identify areas for improvement and ensure compliance with shared standards.

Corrective and Preventive Actions (CAPA): QMS platforms facilitate the CAPA process, allowing partners to jointly address quality issues and track the effectiveness of corrective actions. This ensures continuous improvement and helps prevent recurring problems.

Access Control and Permissions: Collaborative QMS platforms provide role-based access, allowing partners to view relevant data while safeguarding sensitive information. This builds trust while maintaining data security.

3. Establishing Clear Communication Protocols

Clear communication is essential for effective quality collaboration. Miscommunication can lead to errors, misunderstandings, and delays, so establishing communication protocols is key.

Defined Roles and Responsibilities: Clearly outline the roles and responsibilities of each partner in the quality management process. This minimizes confusion and ensures that each party understands their specific duties.

Regular Meetings and Updates: Regular virtual or in-person meetings foster communication and allow partners to discuss quality-related issues, performance metrics, and areas for improvement. Consistent updates create a shared understanding of ongoing challenges and solutions.

Real-Time Communication Tools: Digital communication tools such as video conferencing, instant messaging, and collaborative platforms enhance communication and facilitate immediate responses to quality issues.

4. Aligning Quality Goals and KPIs

Quality collaboration is most effective when all partners work toward shared goals and performance indicators. By aligning quality objectives, companies and their partners can measure success consistently and ensure accountability.

Shared KPIs and Metrics: Identify key performance indicators (KPIs) that measure quality performance across the supply chain, such as defect rates, return rates, and compliance rates. Using shared KPIs promotes alignment and encourages each partner to contribute to quality improvement.

Continuous Tracking and Feedback: Continuous tracking of KPIs provides a clear picture of quality performance. Regular feedback sessions allow partners to discuss performance results, identify areas for improvement, and set new targets.

5. Leveraging Advanced Quality Analytics

Advanced quality analytics, enabled by digital tools, allows companies to gain insights from their quality data and make data-driven decisions.

Analytics can help identify trends, predict potential issues, and optimize quality processes across the supply chain.

Predictive Quality Analytics: Predictive analytics uses historical data and algorithms to forecast potential quality issues. By sharing predictive insights, partners can take proactive measures to prevent defects and improve quality.

Root Cause Analysis (RCA): Conducting RCA jointly with supply chain partners helps identify the underlying causes of recurring quality problems. Advanced analytics tools can facilitate RCA by analyzing data across multiple points in the supply chain, ensuring thorough investigations and effective resolutions.

Performance Benchmarking: Benchmarking quality performance across different suppliers or production facilities helps identify best practices and areas for improvement. It enables partners to compare quality outcomes and adopt practices that yield superior results.

6. Building Trust Through Transparency and Accountability

Trust is essential for successful collaboration. By being transparent and accountable, companies can build strong relationships with their supply chain partners, fostering a culture of mutual respect and shared responsibility.

Open Access to Quality Data: Providing supply chain partners with access to relevant quality data fosters transparency and accountability. Partners can see the quality results of their efforts and understand how their contributions impact overall supply chain performance.

Mutual Accountability Mechanisms: Establishing accountability mechanisms, such as shared quality reviews and audits, ensures that all partners are responsible for quality outcomes. It encourages a culture where everyone takes ownership of quality performance.

Clear Contractual Agreements: Contracts that outline quality expectations, penalties for non-compliance, and rewards for superior quality performance can strengthen accountability. These agreements set clear standards and motivate partners to prioritize quality.

C. Case Studies: Successful Quality Collaboration in Digital Supply Chains

Case Study 1: Apple and Supplier Quality Collaboration

Apple has stringent quality standards and collaborates closely with its suppliers to ensure product excellence. The company uses digital tools to monitor supplier quality, conducts joint audits, and shares real-time performance data with partners. This approach allows Apple to maintain its high-quality standards, reduce defects, and strengthen its supplier relationships.

Case Study 2: Procter & Gamble's Supplier Quality Management System

Procter & Gamble (P&G) has implemented a Supplier Quality Management System that leverages digital tools to share quality data, conduct joint inspections, and track performance metrics with suppliers. By aligning quality goals and establishing regular feedback sessions, P&G ensures consistent quality across its supply chain, fostering long-term partnerships based on mutual trust and accountability.

D. Challenges in Quality Collaboration and How to Address Them

While digital quality collaboration offers numerous benefits, companies may face certain challenges:

Data Privacy Concerns: Sharing quality data with external partners may raise privacy concerns. To address this, companies should use secure platforms, control data access, and comply with data privacy regulations.

Cultural Differences: Differences in corporate culture and quality standards can hinder collaboration. Building a common understanding through regular communication and training can help overcome cultural barriers.

Resistance to Technology: Some partners may resist adopting digital tools for quality collaboration. Offering training and highlighting the benefits of digital tools can encourage technology adoption.

Cost of Implementation: Implementing digital tools for quality management can be costly. To mitigate costs, companies can start with scalable solutions and gradually expand the scope of digital collaboration.

Quality collaboration with supply chain partners is critical in the digital age, where customer expectations and regulatory requirements demand a unified approach to quality management. By leveraging real-time data sharing, advanced analytics, and clear communication protocols, companies can build effective partnerships that promote transparency, reduce risks, and drive continuous improvement. As digital transformation continues to evolve, quality collaboration will play an increasingly central role in ensuring supply chain excellence, helping organizations meet the challenges of a dynamic and interconnected global market.

8. Customer-Centric Quality in the Digital Age

8.1 Customer Expectations in a Digital World

In the digital age, customer expectations have evolved dramatically due to increased connectivity, instant access to information, and heightened competition across industries. Digital transformation has empowered customers with more choices, greater transparency, and higher standards for quality, service, and speed. This shift has required companies to place a stronger emphasis on understanding and meeting customer expectations, as customers today are well-informed, vocal, and highly responsive to brands that offer superior quality and personalized experiences.

This section explores how digital transformation reshapes customer expectations regarding quality, highlighting the demand for speed, personalization, transparency, and continuous improvement.

A. How Digital Transformation is Influencing Customer Expectations

Digital transformation has fundamentally altered the landscape of customer expectations by influencing how customers interact with brands and perceive quality. Some of the key ways in which it has impacted customer expectations are:

Instant Access to Information: With digital channels at their fingertips, customers can easily research products, read reviews, and compare options. This immediate access has heightened customer awareness and demands for quality. Poor reviews or product recalls spread rapidly, emphasizing the importance of quality assurance.

Higher Expectations for Speed and Convenience: The fast-paced nature of the digital age has led to an expectation for speed and convenience. Customers now expect quicker responses, real-time updates, and rapid resolutions for any issues. Companies that fail to deliver on these expectations risk losing customer trust and loyalty.

Personalization and Tailored Experiences: Digital transformation has enabled companies to collect and analyze data, leading to an increased ability to personalize products and services. Customers now expect brands to understand their individual needs, preferences, and behaviors. They seek products that not only meet functional requirements but also align with their lifestyles and values.

Demand for Transparency and Authenticity: Today's customers want to know the details behind the products they purchase, from sourcing materials to manufacturing practices. This emphasis on transparency is particularly strong in industries like food, fashion, and electronics, where sustainability and ethical sourcing are crucial considerations for quality.

Continuous Improvement and Innovation: Customers have become accustomed to frequent updates and innovations, particularly with tech products and digital services. The expectation is that companies will continually improve quality, offer new features, and address any identified issues without delay.

B. Key Aspects of Customer Expectations in the Digital World

To keep pace with digital customer expectations, companies must consider several crucial aspects when designing their quality strategies. These aspects highlight the modern customer's needs and illustrate the demands placed on businesses to provide superior quality and seamless experiences.

1. Quality as a Comprehensive Experience

In the digital age, quality goes beyond the physical attributes of a product; it encompasses the entire customer experience, from the ease of browsing products online to post-purchase customer service. Quality now represents every interaction a customer has with a brand, and poor service at any point in the customer journey can impact the brand's overall perception.

Integrated Quality Management: Quality management now includes every touchpoint a customer interacts with. Companies must integrate quality standards into customer service, logistics, product presentation, and communication to maintain a cohesive experience.

Seamless Omnichannel Experience: Customers expect consistent quality across multiple channels—whether they are shopping online, in-store, or interacting with customer support. Any discrepancy in quality standards across channels can lead to dissatisfaction.

2. Proactive Problem Solving and Responsiveness

In today's fast-paced market, customers expect companies to anticipate potential quality issues and resolve them before they impact the customer experience. Digital tools enable companies to monitor product performance, capture feedback in real time, and address issues immediately.

Proactive Customer Service: Brands are expected to proactively identify and resolve issues before they become problems for customers. This includes notifying customers of potential delays, recalls, or any quality issues affecting their purchases.

24/7 Availability and Immediate Support: With customers spread across different time zones and expecting immediate assistance, companies are leveraging AI-powered chatbots, automated responses, and customer service platforms to deliver round-the-clock support.

3. Personalization and Customization

Personalization has become a critical aspect of customer expectations, driven by the capabilities of digital transformation to collect and analyze customer data. Today's customers value products and services that cater to their individual preferences and lifestyle, making personalization a key factor in perceived quality.

Customized Product Offerings: Companies that use customer data to offer tailored product recommendations, sizes, or configurations align more closely with customer needs, thereby enhancing the quality perception.

Personalized Interactions: Personalization extends to how companies interact with customers. Using customer data to tailor communication and engagement helps customers feel valued and understood, fostering a stronger connection to the brand.

4. Real-Time Feedback and Instant Gratification

Customers now expect immediate feedback on their queries, complaints, and concerns. Social media, mobile apps, and online reviews provide customers with platforms to share their experiences instantaneously, influencing others and amplifying the impact of customer feedback.

Instant Feedback Mechanisms: Companies that facilitate real-time feedback through surveys, chat options, or direct messages can respond to issues quickly and resolve them effectively, thereby boosting customer satisfaction.

Public Response to Feedback: Digital platforms allow companies to showcase their responsiveness to customer concerns publicly. A quick, thoughtful response can improve the brand's image, whereas a delayed or inadequate response may damage its reputation.

5. Ethical and Sustainable Practices

Customers today value companies that prioritize ethical practices and sustainability. Digital transparency has empowered customers to research and scrutinize a company's practices, including how products are sourced, manufactured, and distributed.

Ethical Sourcing and Production: Many customers consider ethical sourcing and environmentally friendly practices part of product quality. Companies that uphold and communicate these values align more closely with customer expectations, fostering loyalty and trust.

Environmental Responsibility: Digital transparency enables companies to showcase their sustainability initiatives, such as waste reduction, eco-friendly materials, and energy-efficient practices. Customers increasingly see such efforts as essential components of product quality.

C. Strategies for Meeting Evolving Customer Expectations

To keep up with modern customer expectations, companies must adopt a customer-centric quality approach that is proactive, responsive, and aligned with digital transformation initiatives. Here are some strategies to help companies meet these evolving expectations:

1. Implementing Customer-Centric Quality Metrics

Traditional quality metrics may not capture the full scope of today's customer expectations. Companies need to redefine their quality metrics to focus on customer satisfaction, responsiveness, and experience.

Customer Satisfaction Scores (CSAT): These scores reflect customer satisfaction levels and provide insights into areas that need improvement. CSAT scores can be measured after key interactions, such as purchases, customer service calls, or product returns.

Net Promoter Score (NPS): NPS measures customer loyalty by asking customers how likely they are to recommend the product or service. It provides a clear indicator of overall satisfaction and quality perception.

Real-Time Quality Monitoring: Leveraging digital tools to monitor quality in real time helps companies track issues, gauge performance, and respond promptly to changing customer needs.

2. Leveraging AI for Predictive Quality Management

Artificial intelligence (AI) is a game-changer in proactive quality management. AI-powered analytics can identify patterns in customer feedback, detect quality issues early, and recommend solutions to prevent issues from reaching customers.

Sentiment Analysis for Customer Feedback: AI can analyze customer feedback, including social media posts, online reviews, and customer support interactions, to understand sentiment and identify recurring issues. This information helps companies address problems before they escalate.

Predictive Maintenance for Product Quality: For companies with physical products, AI can predict when maintenance or repairs might be needed, reducing the likelihood of product failures and ensuring customers receive high-quality items.

3. Utilizing Big Data for Customer Insights

Big data analytics enables companies to understand customer behavior, preferences, and trends, allowing them to tailor quality efforts to meet customer expectations. Analyzing big data provides actionable insights that drive better decision-making and product development.

Understanding Customer Preferences: Big data reveals preferences and buying patterns, allowing companies to refine products based on customer insights. This improves the alignment between products and customer needs, enhancing quality perception.

Continuous Quality Improvement: Data-driven insights highlight areas for improvement across the customer journey, from product design to after-sales support, enabling companies to continuously optimize their offerings.

4. Enhancing Transparency with Blockchain

Blockchain technology offers a transparent and secure way to document product origins, quality checks, and supply chain processes. This transparency builds trust with customers who seek assurance about product authenticity and ethical practices.

Traceability in the Supply Chain: Blockchain enables companies to track and verify the journey of products across the supply chain. Customers can view the origin, handling, and quality certifications of products, ensuring they meet their expectations for transparency.

Ensuring Authenticity and Compliance: Blockchain provides an immutable record of product information, offering customers confidence in product authenticity, quality, and compliance with industry standards.

In a digital world, customers have elevated expectations for quality, speed, personalization, transparency, and sustainability. Digital transformation has reshaped how customers perceive quality and interact with brands, demanding a new level of responsiveness, proactive quality management, and ethical responsibility. To thrive in this environment, companies must embrace a customer-centric approach, leveraging digital tools and data to meet evolving expectations and deliver a quality experience that resonates with modern consumers. By understanding and anticipating these expectations, companies can strengthen customer loyalty, build brand equity, and maintain a competitive edge in today's rapidly changing marketplace.

8.2 Leveraging Customer Feedback and Social Media

In the digital age, customer feedback has become an invaluable asset for organizations aiming to improve their products, services, and overall quality standards. Social media and other digital platforms have transformed how businesses gather and analyze customer feedback, making it possible to receive real-time insights directly from users. By leveraging feedback from social media, companies can stay attuned to customer sentiment, address issues promptly, and continuously improve quality to meet evolving expectations. This section explores the power of real-time feedback loops, social listening, and the strategic use of social media for enhancing quality management.

A. The Power of Real-Time Feedback Loops

Real-time feedback loops allow companies to receive instant responses from customers regarding their experiences, preferences, and complaints. Unlike traditional feedback mechanisms that may take days or weeks, digital platforms offer immediate feedback, enabling companies to respond quickly and effectively.

1. Immediate Insight into Customer Experiences

Incorporating real-time feedback loops into quality management provides immediate insights into customer satisfaction levels and areas for improvement. This enables companies to react to problems as they arise, rather than discovering them through delayed feedback or data analysis.

Quick Response to Quality Issues: Real-time feedback allows organizations to respond to quality concerns immediately. For instance, if customers report product defects, customer service can initiate corrective actions or recalls as needed.

Enhanced Customer Satisfaction: Responding to feedback promptly demonstrates a commitment to customer satisfaction. When customers see that their input is valued and addressed, they are more likely to remain loyal to the brand.

2. Continuous Improvement through Ongoing Feedback

Continuous feedback helps create a cycle of ongoing improvement where customer input directly influences quality management strategies. By keeping an open line of communication, companies can make incremental changes that gradually improve their offerings.

Data-Driven Decision-Making: Regular feedback provides a constant stream of data that can guide decision-making in product design, service offerings, and customer service. Companies can adjust based on real-time insights, creating a more adaptable quality management approach.

Reduced Product Development Time: Real-time feedback during product testing phases allows companies to identify potential issues early on. This reduces time-to-market, as issues are resolved quickly, and products are refined based on real-time customer feedback.

3. Creating Transparent Feedback Channels

Encouraging customers to provide feedback requires establishing accessible, user-friendly channels. This transparency helps customers feel comfortable sharing their thoughts and opinions, ultimately enhancing the quality management process.

In-App Feedback Tools: Many companies integrate feedback tools directly into their websites, mobile apps, and other digital platforms, making it easy for customers to share their experiences without leaving the interface.

Automated Feedback Collection: Automated surveys sent after specific interactions, such as purchases or customer service calls, can gather valuable insights with minimal effort from the customer.

B. Social Listening for Quality Management

Social listening is the process of monitoring social media platforms and other digital channels for mentions of a company, product, or service. By paying attention to these conversations, companies can gather insights that help improve quality and strengthen customer relationships.

1. Understanding Customer Sentiment and Trends

Social listening provides a window into customer sentiment, revealing how customers feel about a brand and its products. This approach helps companies identify trends, preferences, and emerging quality issues that may require attention.

Sentiment Analysis: Tools that analyze social media comments can determine whether customer sentiment is positive, neutral, or negative. These insights help companies understand general feelings toward their offerings and uncover areas for improvement.

Identifying Quality Trends: Social listening can reveal trends in customer expectations and perceptions. For example, if multiple customers express a desire for eco-friendly packaging, a company may choose to prioritize this change to enhance quality perception.

2. Proactive Quality Control through Social Monitoring

Social listening allows companies to be proactive rather than reactive in their quality management strategies. By identifying potential issues early on, businesses can address them before they escalate.

Early Detection of Product Issues: When customers report issues on social media, companies can take note and investigate the problem. This proactive approach helps companies address concerns early, avoiding potential recalls or widespread dissatisfaction.

Timely Product or Service Improvements: If customers frequently mention specific product flaws or service challenges, companies can prioritize these areas for improvement, ensuring quality aligns with customer expectations.

3. Benchmarking against Competitors

Social listening also provides insights into competitors, as customers may discuss multiple brands on the same platforms. Monitoring these conversations can help companies identify strengths and weaknesses relative to their competitors.

Identifying Competitor Strengths: By understanding what customers appreciate about competitors, companies can incorporate similar qualities into their products or services.

Spotting Market Opportunities: Social listening reveals unmet customer needs that companies can address to differentiate their offerings from those of competitors, enhancing overall quality perception.

C. Implementing Effective Social Media Feedback Systems

Using social media as a source of feedback for quality improvement involves creating a well-structured system that enables the collection, analysis, and application of customer feedback.

1. Engaging Customers Directly on Social Media

Social media enables direct interaction with customers, allowing companies to foster a sense of community and encourage open dialogue about quality concerns.

Real-Time Customer Support: Many companies use social media channels for customer support, allowing customers to report issues and ask questions. Responding quickly to concerns on these platforms demonstrates a commitment to quality and customer satisfaction.

Encouraging Open Feedback: Companies can actively seek feedback on social media by posting questions, running polls, or inviting customers to share their thoughts. Engaging customers directly helps companies gain a better understanding of their needs and preferences.

2. Utilizing Analytics for Insights

To make the most of social media feedback, companies should leverage analytics tools that track and analyze customer feedback across different platforms. This data enables a more structured approach to quality management.

Aggregating Customer Feedback: Analytics tools can collect feedback from various social media channels, creating a centralized source of information for quality analysis. Aggregating feedback helps companies detect patterns and common concerns more effectively.

Analyzing Feedback by Demographics: Social media analytics can segment customer feedback by demographics, enabling companies to understand how quality perceptions vary among different customer groups and adjust accordingly.

3. Establishing Key Performance Indicators (KPIs) for Social Feedback

To measure the effectiveness of social media feedback systems, companies can establish KPIs that align with quality management goals. These indicators help assess whether social listening efforts contribute to quality improvements.

Customer Satisfaction Score (CSAT): This KPI tracks customer satisfaction levels based on feedback received through social media channels. High CSAT scores indicate that social media feedback aligns with customer expectations.

Response Time and Resolution Rate: Measuring how quickly and effectively issues reported on social media are addressed helps companies gauge their responsiveness, which is a crucial factor in customer satisfaction.

D. Case Studies: Successful Use of Social Media Feedback for Quality Improvement

Several companies have effectively used social media feedback to enhance their quality management strategies, resulting in increased customer satisfaction and loyalty.

Case Study 1: Starbucks' "My Starbucks Idea" Platform

In 2008, Starbucks launched the "My Starbucks Idea" platform, allowing customers to submit ideas, vote on suggestions, and share feedback about the company's products and services. This initiative allowed Starbucks to capture customer ideas directly from its user base and incorporate them into its offerings.

Crowdsourced Quality Improvements: Through the platform, Starbucks gathered over 150,000 ideas, leading to product innovations and improvements, such as the introduction of new menu items and updated store designs.

Enhanced Customer Loyalty: By giving customers a voice in its decision-making process, Starbucks strengthened its customer relationships and demonstrated a commitment to quality improvement based on user input.

Case Study 2: Netflix and Real-Time Social Listening

Netflix uses social media feedback to assess audience sentiment and identify content preferences. By monitoring conversations about shows, Netflix gains insights into what resonates with viewers and uses this information to shape its content offerings.

Content Curation Based on Audience Feedback: When Netflix released a show that received poor feedback, it was able to take quick action by recommending similar shows that better aligned with audience interests, reducing churn and improving viewer satisfaction.

Continuous Improvement in Customer Experience: Netflix's social listening efforts allow the company to continuously adjust its content strategy based on viewer preferences, thereby improving customer satisfaction and loyalty.

Leveraging customer feedback and social media for quality improvement enables companies to understand customer needs, address quality issues in real time, and enhance customer satisfaction. Real-time feedback loops create a continuous improvement cycle, while social listening provides valuable insights into customer sentiment, competitor performance, and market trends. By engaging customers directly, analyzing social feedback, and applying these insights to quality management strategies, companies can stay competitive, responsive, and in tune with customer expectations in today's digital world. In this way, companies can foster a customer-centric quality approach that strengthens relationships, builds trust, and delivers an exceptional experience that meets and exceeds modern quality standards.

8.3 Digital Tools for Measuring Customer Satisfaction

In a customer-centric digital landscape, measuring customer satisfaction is essential for ensuring that products and services meet customer expectations. Digital tools have become invaluable in this process, providing companies with precise, real-time insights into customer satisfaction levels. Common tools like the Net Promoter Score (NPS), Customer Satisfaction Score (CSAT), and digital surveys offer effective ways to gauge satisfaction, track trends over time, and make data-driven quality improvements. This section explores how these tools contribute to quality management, the benefits of each approach, and strategies for integrating them into a comprehensive customer satisfaction measurement system.

A. The Importance of Measuring Customer Satisfaction Digitally

Understanding customer satisfaction is more critical than ever, as the digital age has reshaped expectations and heightened competition across industries. Digital tools for measuring satisfaction offer numerous advantages:

Real-Time Feedback: Digital tools allow businesses to collect and analyze feedback almost instantly, enabling quick responses to customer needs or issues.

Data-Driven Decision-Making: With quantitative insights, companies can make informed decisions that directly impact quality, aligning improvements with customer desires.

Improved Customer Retention: Monitoring satisfaction and acting on feedback demonstrates a commitment to quality, increasing customer loyalty and retention.

By using digital measurement tools, organizations can stay attuned to customer preferences and ensure that they are meeting or exceeding quality standards in real time.

B. Net Promoter Score (NPS)

The Net Promoter Score (NPS) is a widely used metric for measuring customer loyalty and satisfaction. NPS gauges how likely customers are to recommend a company's product or service, providing a simple yet powerful indication of overall customer sentiment.

1. Understanding NPS

NPS is calculated by asking customers a single question: "How likely are you to recommend our product/service to others on a scale of 0 to 10?" Respondents are then grouped into three categories:

Promoters (scores 9–10): Loyal customers who are highly satisfied and likely to recommend the product or service.

Passives (scores 7–8): Customers who are satisfied but may not be as loyal or enthusiastic.

Detractors (scores 0–6): Customers who are unhappy and may discourage others from using the product or service.

The NPS score is calculated by subtracting the percentage of Detractors from the percentage of Promoters.

2. Benefits of NPS for Quality Management

NPS offers valuable insights into customer satisfaction that are directly linked to loyalty and retention. Key benefits include:

Simple and Actionable: NPS is straightforward to measure and interpret, making it easy for companies to track customer satisfaction over time and identify trends.

Predictive of Business Growth: NPS is often used as a leading indicator of growth, as it reflects customer loyalty and potential for organic recommendations.

Segmented Feedback: Companies can analyze NPS by demographics, purchase history, or other variables to gain deeper insights into specific customer segments.

3. Using NPS for Continuous Improvement

Incorporating NPS into quality management helps organizations identify strengths and weaknesses, allowing for targeted quality improvements. For instance:

Addressing Detractor Feedback: Companies can follow up with Detractors to understand their pain points and implement changes to address common issues.

Leveraging Promoter Insights: Promoters' positive experiences can be studied to identify practices or features that should be emphasized or expanded.

C. Customer Satisfaction Score (CSAT)

The Customer Satisfaction Score (CSAT) is another essential metric, focusing on measuring specific customer interactions or experiences. It is widely used to evaluate short-term satisfaction, providing immediate insights into how customers feel about recent engagements with a company.

1. Understanding CSAT

CSAT is usually measured by asking customers to rate their satisfaction with a product, service, or experience on a scale from 1 to 5 (or 1 to

10). The CSAT score is calculated by dividing the number of positive responses (e.g., scores 4 and 5) by the total number of responses and then converting this ratio into a percentage.

For example:

CSAT Question: "How satisfied are you with your recent purchase?"

Scale: Responses range from very dissatisfied to very satisfied, with only the top ratings counted as positive.

2. Benefits of CSAT for Quality Management

CSAT is effective for evaluating customer satisfaction in specific areas, making it ideal for organizations that want to pinpoint quality improvements in particular aspects of their operations.

Focused on Specific Experiences: CSAT scores provide targeted feedback on specific interactions, helping companies identify exact points of satisfaction or dissatisfaction.

Immediate Actionability: Because CSAT captures satisfaction right after a customer interaction, companies can address issues quickly to prevent future dissatisfaction.

Versatile Use: CSAT can be used across various touchpoints, including customer service interactions, product purchases, and post-service evaluations.

3. Using CSAT to Improve Quality Management

By analyzing CSAT data, organizations can improve quality in areas that impact immediate customer satisfaction.

Enhancing Customer Support: If CSAT scores are low for customer support, companies can focus on training or process changes to improve service quality.

Improving Product Features: CSAT feedback on product satisfaction can inform product development, helping companies prioritize features or resolve common complaints.

D. Digital Surveys for Comprehensive Feedback

Digital surveys are versatile tools that enable companies to gather in-depth feedback on customer experiences. While NPS and CSAT provide quick snapshots, digital surveys allow for more detailed responses, capturing a range of perspectives on quality.

1. Types of Digital Surveys

Digital surveys can be customized for various objectives, offering flexibility in gathering insights:

Post-Purchase Surveys: These surveys assess satisfaction with a product or service immediately after purchase, providing feedback on recent customer experiences.

Periodic Satisfaction Surveys: Sent on a scheduled basis (e.g., quarterly or annually), these surveys gauge overall satisfaction and can highlight trends in customer perceptions over time.

Customized Quality Surveys: These surveys target specific areas, such as product features, service quality, or support satisfaction, enabling organizations to collect focused feedback.

2. Benefits of Digital Surveys for Quality Management

Digital surveys provide a comprehensive view of customer satisfaction, helping companies understand both high-level trends and specific quality issues.

Detailed Insights: Unlike single-question metrics, surveys can include multiple questions, offering a broader understanding of customer opinions.

Quantitative and Qualitative Data: Surveys can capture both quantitative ratings and open-ended feedback, providing a richer picture of customer experiences.

Easily Scalable: Digital surveys can be sent to a large audience quickly, making them an efficient way to gather customer input across regions or demographics.

3. Leveraging Survey Data for Quality Improvements

Survey data can reveal specific areas for quality enhancement and allow for proactive decision-making.

Analyzing Trends Over Time: Periodic surveys can help companies track changes in customer satisfaction and gauge the effectiveness of quality improvement initiatives.

Segmenting Responses by Customer Type: Companies can analyze survey responses by customer segment (e.g., new vs. returning customers) to identify unique needs and tailor quality strategies.

Informing Product and Service Development: Open-ended survey responses often reveal new ideas for product features or service improvements, giving companies actionable insights for quality advancement.

E. Integrating NPS, CSAT, and Digital Surveys for Holistic Quality Management

While each tool has its strengths, combining NPS, CSAT, and digital surveys creates a comprehensive approach to measuring customer satisfaction. This integrated approach allows companies to capture both general sentiment and specific feedback, ensuring a well-rounded understanding of customer satisfaction levels.

1. Building a Comprehensive Measurement System

To maximize the effectiveness of customer satisfaction tools, companies should establish a systematic approach that combines the unique benefits of each:

Using NPS for Brand-Level Insights: NPS provides a broad view of loyalty and overall satisfaction, which can help shape company-wide quality initiatives.

Employing CSAT for Immediate Feedback: CSAT scores can highlight specific issues or areas needing prompt attention, helping companies address quality at a granular level.

Utilizing Surveys for In-Depth Analysis: Surveys enable companies to dive deeper into customer preferences, uncovering actionable insights for long-term quality improvements.

2. Leveraging Data from Multiple Touchpoints

An integrated system also allows companies to collect feedback from multiple customer touchpoints, painting a comprehensive picture of customer satisfaction:

Aggregating Data for a Unified View: By combining data from NPS, CSAT, and surveys, companies can create a centralized repository of customer feedback, allowing for cross-functional analysis and strategy alignment.

Tracking Performance across Channels: Monitoring customer satisfaction across various channels (e.g., online, in-store, customer support) helps identify areas where quality may differ, allowing for channel-specific improvements.

3. Ensuring Continuous Quality Improvement

An integrated approach to customer satisfaction measurement supports a cycle of continuous improvement. By regularly reviewing and acting on feedback, companies can adapt their quality management strategies to changing customer expectations.

Digital tools like NPS, CSAT, and digital surveys offer valuable insights into customer satisfaction, providing a data-driven foundation for quality management in the digital age. Each tool contributes a unique perspective on customer experience, from broad loyalty insights to specific feedback on individual interactions. By integrating these tools into a cohesive measurement system, companies can create a holistic approach to customer satisfaction, driving continuous improvement and delivering products and services that meet—and exceed—customer expectations.

9. Agile Quality Management

The evolving business landscape, marked by rapid technological advancements and shifting consumer expectations, has pushed organizations to embrace agile methodologies across various functions, including quality management. Agile quality management applies the principles of agile—originally developed for software development—to the processes that ensure product or service quality. This approach prioritizes flexibility, customer collaboration, and iterative improvement, offering a dynamic contrast to traditional quality management methods.

In this section, we explore agile quality management, beginning with an introduction to agile principles in quality and a comparison with traditional approaches.

9.1 Introduction to Agile Principles in Quality

Agile quality management aligns with the core principles of agility: responsiveness to change, frequent feedback, and incremental improvement. By integrating these principles into quality processes, organizations can maintain high-quality standards while adapting quickly to new requirements or customer feedback. This approach is particularly valuable in fast-paced industries, where time-to-market and the ability to adjust to customer needs are critical for success.

Core Agile Principles in Quality Management

Agile quality management incorporates key agile principles, reshaping the traditional approach in a way that supports flexibility and efficiency:

Customer Collaboration over Contract Negotiation: In agile quality, close collaboration with customers or end-users is prioritized. Quality teams work to ensure that customer feedback is continuously integrated into the product or service, leading to outcomes that closely align with customer expectations.

Responding to Change over Following a Plan: Agile quality management allows for continuous adjustment in response to new information or shifting market needs. This means that quality processes are flexible and can evolve throughout the product lifecycle.

Frequent Delivery of Value: Agile emphasizes delivering small, functional components of a product frequently, which allows quality teams to test and evaluate each component as it's produced. This approach ensures quality at every stage rather than solely at the end.

Continuous Improvement: Agile teams are committed to iterative improvement, consistently refining both the product and the quality processes. Agile quality management includes regular retrospectives to review what went well and what could be improved, driving ongoing optimization.

Empowered Cross-Functional Teams: Agile teams are typically cross-functional and empowered to make decisions, which enables faster responses to issues or defects. In agile quality management, cross-functional collaboration is essential for ensuring that quality is maintained across all aspects of the product or service.

Differences between Traditional and Agile Quality Management Approaches

Agile quality management represents a significant departure from traditional quality management approaches, which are often characterized by linear processes, extensive documentation, and predefined standards. Here's how the two approaches differ:

Aspect	Traditional Quality Management	Agile Quality Management
Process Flow	Linear, sequential (often using models like PDCA)	Iterative, continuous feedback and adaptation
Documentation	Emphasizes detailed documentation	Focuses on essential documentation, prioritizing real-time updates
Customer Involvement	Limited, primarily at predefined stages	Continuous collaboration and frequent feedback
Flexibility	Limited adaptability: changes can be costly	Highly adaptable: changes are expected and managed flexibly
Quality Checks	Primarily at the end of each phase or project	Continuous quality checks integrated throughout development
Improvement Focus	Improvement is periodic, often after project completion	Continuous improvement with regular retrospectives

Traditional quality management often adheres to strict standards, requiring extensive testing and validation phases that may delay the feedback loop. Agile quality management, on the other hand, integrates quality assessments and feedback continuously, reducing the time to implement improvements.

Benefits of Agile Quality Management

Adopting agile quality management offers several advantages, particularly in environments where change is frequent or customer expectations are dynamic:

Enhanced Responsiveness to Change: Agile quality management allows teams to adapt quality processes quickly in response to evolving requirements, reducing the time needed to incorporate changes.

Higher Customer Satisfaction: Frequent customer collaboration and iterative improvements ensure that the final product meets or exceeds customer expectations.

Reduced Time to Market: Agile quality management enables faster detection and resolution of issues, allowing products to reach the market sooner without compromising on quality.

Improved Cross-Functional Collaboration: Agile teams work closely across departments, resulting in a more cohesive approach to quality that considers multiple perspectives and expertise.

Continuous Improvement: Agile emphasizes regular retrospectives, which help teams identify opportunities for improvement, ensuring that quality processes are constantly optimized.

Challenges of Implementing Agile Quality Management

While agile quality management offers numerous benefits, it also presents challenges, especially for organizations accustomed to traditional methods. Key challenges include:

Cultural Shift: Moving from a traditional to an agile approach requires a mindset shift across the organization, which can be challenging to implement without strong leadership and change management.

Training and Skill Development: Quality teams may need training in agile methodologies and tools to fully embrace the agile approach.

Balancing Speed and Quality: Agile's emphasis on speed can sometimes conflict with quality standards, requiring careful management to maintain high-quality outcomes.

Customer Involvement: Agile quality management requires consistent customer input, which may be difficult to obtain, particularly for certain products or services.

Complexity in Scaling: While agile works well for smaller teams, scaling agile quality management across large organizations can be complex, requiring alignment across departments and consistent practices.

Applying Agile Quality Management: Key Strategies

To effectively implement agile quality management, organizations can leverage several strategies:

Cross-Functional Teams: Agile quality requires diverse skills and perspectives, so organizations should assemble cross-functional teams that can address quality from all angles, including customer service, product development, and production.

Frequent Iterations and Feedback: Regular iterations allow teams to evaluate quality continuously, ensuring that each iteration meets quality standards before moving on to the next.

Automated Testing: Automated testing tools can enhance agile quality management by providing fast, consistent feedback on quality. Automated tests help teams quickly identify issues, reducing manual work and improving accuracy.

Real-Time Communication and Collaboration Tools: Agile quality teams rely on tools that support fast, transparent communication. Digital platforms such as Slack, Jira, and Trello facilitate quick feedback and updates, enabling teams to respond promptly to quality issues.

Regular Retrospectives: Agile quality management includes retrospectives to review each iteration and identify areas for improvement. This practice fosters a culture of continuous improvement, helping teams refine quality processes over time.

Case Study: Agile Quality Management in Practice

Company X was facing challenges with its traditional quality management approach, particularly in keeping up with rapid changes in customer demands. After transitioning to an agile quality management framework, Company X experienced significant improvements in customer satisfaction and product quality.

Cross-Functional Collaboration: By forming agile, cross-functional teams, Company X was able to streamline its quality processes, reducing the time to identify and address issues.

Iterative Feedback: The company implemented frequent testing and feedback loops, enabling the team to make adjustments based on real-time customer feedback.

Automated Testing: By adopting automated testing, Company X reduced errors, cut down on repetitive tasks, and freed up resources to focus on continuous quality improvements.

After implementing agile quality management, Company X not only saw faster production times but also achieved higher product quality, proving that agile methods can be highly effective for quality management in dynamic industries.

Agile quality management represents a transformative approach that empowers organizations to meet changing customer expectations and deliver high-quality products in less time. By integrating agile principles—such as customer collaboration, flexibility, and continuous improvement—into quality processes, companies can build a responsive, efficient system that aligns closely with both market demands and internal goals.

Although agile quality management may be challenging to implement, the benefits, including enhanced responsiveness, improved customer satisfaction, and faster time-to-market, make it a valuable strategy for organizations seeking to innovate and lead in competitive markets. As organizations continue to evolve, agile quality management will play an increasingly critical role in achieving and sustaining excellence in quality.

9.2 Applying Agile Techniques to Quality Management

Agile techniques, initially developed for software development, have expanded beyond their original domain and are now applied across a wide range of industries and functions, including quality management. In quality management, agile techniques emphasize flexibility, iterative improvements, and customer-centric practices that help organizations respond to rapid changes, improve efficiency, and maintain high-quality standards. This approach is particularly valuable in environments with fluctuating customer expectations, dynamic market trends, or fast-paced production cycles.

In this section, we delve into how agile methodologies can be applied to quality management, including key principles and techniques such as iterative improvements, feedback loops, and flexible practices that help maintain and enhance quality standards.

Agile Methodologies in Quality Management

Agile methodologies in quality management rely on breaking down quality assurance processes into smaller, manageable tasks that can be completed in iterations, allowing for continuous assessment and refinement. By embedding quality checks at each stage of development or production, quality teams can identify and address issues early, resulting in a more streamlined and effective process.

Key Agile Methodologies Applied to Quality Management

Scrum: Scrum is one of the most widely used agile methodologies, particularly in software development, and it can be effectively adapted for quality management. In a Scrum-based approach, quality management tasks are organized into short, time-bound cycles called "sprints." Each sprint includes planning, execution, and review phases. By incorporating quality checks and testing within each sprint, teams can continuously improve quality throughout the project lifecycle.

Daily Stand-ups: Teams hold short, daily meetings (stand-ups) to discuss progress, challenges, and plans for the day. This keeps quality management aligned with overall project goals and provides an opportunity for immediate feedback on any quality issues that arise.

Sprint Reviews: At the end of each sprint, teams review what was achieved, including any quality improvements made during that period. This retrospective process encourages continuous refinement and helps teams identify and address recurring quality challenges.

Kanban: Kanban, a visual management tool, is another agile methodology that is highly adaptable to quality management. Kanban boards allow teams to visualize quality tasks, track their progress, and limit the number of tasks in progress to avoid overloading. This helps teams maintain a steady workflow and focus on quality-related tasks in **a manageable, organized manner.**

Visual Tracking of Quality Tasks: By categorizing quality tasks (e.g., "To Do," "In Progress," "Done"), Kanban boards offer a clear visual of where quality efforts are needed most, enabling teams to allocate resources effectively.

Limiting Work-in-Progress: Kanban's work-in-progress (WIP) limits ensure that quality tasks are completed before new ones begin, reducing bottlenecks and improving focus on current tasks.

Lean and Continuous Improvement (Kaizen): Lean principles focus on minimizing waste and enhancing value, which aligns well with quality management objectives. Techniques such as Kaizen (continuous improvement) are widely used in quality management to create a culture of ongoing refinement and optimization.

Value Stream Mapping: This Lean tool allows quality teams to map out the entire process and identify areas where waste occurs or quality could be improved. It promotes a holistic view of the production or service process, helping teams pinpoint specific stages where quality interventions can have the greatest impact.

Kaizen Events: Quality management can benefit from periodic Kaizen events, where team members collaborate on focused, short-term projects aimed at solving specific quality issues. These events lead to actionable improvements that are implemented and assessed quickly.

XP (Extreme Programming): Although originally designed for software, XP's principles, like continuous testing and close collaboration with stakeholders, can be adapted to quality management. For example, quality teams can adopt XP's emphasis on continuous feedback and testing, implementing practices that enable them to catch and fix issues at each stage of the production cycle.

Continuous Testing: XP's focus on continuous testing is useful for quality management, as it ensures that issues are detected and resolved before they compound. This helps teams maintain high standards throughout the production process.

Stakeholder Collaboration: Engaging customers or stakeholders in the quality review process enables more accurate feedback, leading to improvements that better align with end-user expectations.

Iterative Improvements in Quality Management

Iterative improvement is a cornerstone of agile methodologies and involves making incremental changes that gradually enhance the quality of products or services. This approach differs from traditional quality management, which often emphasizes large-scale changes or periodic quality reviews. Instead, iterative improvement allows teams to test, learn, and apply insights continuously, enabling them to respond quickly to new quality challenges.

The Benefits of Iterative Improvement

Faster Detection and Resolution of Quality Issues: By implementing small, manageable changes regularly, teams can detect and resolve quality issues before they escalate. This minimizes the risk of larger quality failures and reduces the need for rework.

Enhanced Flexibility: Iterative improvement enables quality teams to pivot quickly in response to emerging challenges or new customer requirements. This flexibility is essential in dynamic environments where quality standards may need to adapt to changes in technology, regulations, or market expectations.

Real-Time Feedback: Iterative improvements allow quality teams to receive feedback continuously, rather than waiting until the end of a production cycle. This feedback loop helps teams validate their approaches and adjust their strategies as needed.

Techniques for Implementing Iterative Improvements

Plan-Do-Check-Act (PDCA) Cycle: The PDCA cycle is a classic quality management tool that aligns well with agile iterative improvement. In each cycle, teams plan an improvement, implement it, assess its effectiveness, and act on what they learned to refine the process further.

Quality Reviews and Retrospectives: After each iteration, quality teams can hold retrospectives to discuss successes, challenges, and areas for improvement. This creates a structured opportunity to identify lessons learned and implement further refinements.

Incremental Quality Checks: Instead of conducting quality checks only at the end of a process, agile quality management integrates these checks at each iteration. This helps teams ensure that quality standards are upheld throughout the production process.

Flexibility in Quality Management

Agile quality management emphasizes flexibility, allowing quality teams to adapt their processes as conditions change. This flexibility is crucial in industries where customer preferences, regulatory standards, or production technologies are constantly evolving. By adopting a flexible approach to quality, organizations can maintain high standards without becoming bogged down by rigid processes.

Key Elements of Flexibility in Quality Management

Adaptable Quality Standards: In an agile environment, quality standards may need to be revised based on changing customer needs or regulatory updates. Agile quality teams can quickly adapt their processes to meet new requirements, ensuring that products remain compliant and competitive.

Modular Quality Processes: By designing modular quality processes, teams can adjust specific parts of the process without overhauling the entire system. This allows for targeted changes that respond to particular issues or requirements without disrupting the overall workflow.

Cross-Functional Collaboration: Flexibility is enhanced through collaboration across departments, including production, design, and customer support. This allows quality teams to draw on diverse expertise and make well-rounded adjustments to quality processes.

Real-Time Data and Analytics: Access to real-time data is essential for flexible quality management, as it enables teams to identify and respond to quality issues as they arise. Advanced analytics tools can provide insights that guide decision-making, helping teams focus on areas that need improvement.

Applying agile techniques to quality management introduces a new level of adaptability, efficiency, and responsiveness. By adopting agile methodologies such as Scrum, Kanban, Lean, and XP, quality teams can create iterative, flexible processes that prioritize continuous improvement and customer satisfaction. This approach not only enhances the organization's ability to meet quality standards but also allows it to respond effectively to changing market conditions and customer expectations.

With agile quality management, organizations are better equipped to deliver high-quality products and services in a timely manner. The iterative improvements and flexibility afforded by agile methodologies make them particularly suited to today's fast-paced business environment, ensuring that quality remains a central focus even as companies adapt to new challenges and opportunities.

9.3 Quality Management in Digital Product Development

In the digital age, quality management practices in software and digital product development have had to evolve significantly to keep up with rapid changes in technology, market demands, and user expectations. Agile methodologies and digital tools have become essential in ensuring that digital products, particularly software, meet high standards of quality and user satisfaction.

This section examines quality management in the context of digital product development, emphasizing the role of agile quality management and the benefits it brings to the development of software and digital products. We will also look at case studies that illustrate how companies have successfully implemented agile quality management practices to deliver high-quality digital products.

Agile Quality Management in Digital Product Development

In digital product development, agile quality management is integral to meeting user needs and maintaining competitiveness. Agile methodologies, with their focus on iteration, flexibility, and continuous improvement, align well with the fast-paced, often unpredictable nature of digital product development. Agile quality management ensures that digital products are released with fewer bugs, higher user satisfaction, and a more efficient development process.

Key Components of Agile Quality Management in Digital Development

Incremental Development and Continuous Testing: Agile development is inherently incremental, breaking down projects into smaller, manageable chunks, or iterations. Quality assurance (QA) and testing are performed continuously throughout these iterations, allowing for the early detection and resolution of issues. This helps to reduce the risk of critical errors in the final product and shortens development cycles.

Cross-Functional Teams and Collaboration: Agile methodologies emphasize the importance of cross-functional teams that bring together developers, designers, product managers, and QA specialists. This approach ensures that quality is embedded from the outset of product development, with QA insights being considered alongside feature design and development.

Rapid Feedback Loops: One of the central benefits of agile quality management is the incorporation of rapid feedback loops. By engaging users, stakeholders, and team members in frequent feedback cycles, teams can quickly adjust the product based on real user feedback. This helps prevent issues from escalating and ensures the product aligns with customer needs.

Automated Testing and Deployment: Automation plays a crucial role in agile quality management for digital products. Automated testing tools allow teams to run tests more frequently and cover more scenarios, while continuous integration and continuous deployment (CI/CD) tools help speed up the deployment of new updates. This minimizes the risk of human error and ensures consistency in testing and deployment.

User-Centric Focus: Agile quality management in digital product development often places a strong emphasis on user-centric design and testing. This includes usability testing, performance testing, and user experience (UX) assessments to ensure that the digital product not only functions correctly but also delivers a positive experience to the end user.

Case Studies in Agile Quality Management for Software and Digital Products

To illustrate the effectiveness of agile quality management in digital product development, let's examine some case studies of companies that have successfully implemented these practices.

Case Study 1: Spotify – Continuous Improvement and Agile Quality Management

Spotify, a leading music streaming platform, has grown by adopting an agile approach known as the Spotify Model, which prioritizes flexibility, autonomy, and continuous improvement.

Autonomous Squads: Spotify's development is organized into autonomous squads that operate as cross-functional teams responsible for specific aspects of the product, such as playlist recommendations or user experience features. Each squad is responsible for its own quality assurance processes, allowing for more focused, agile quality management tailored to the squad's objectives.

Continuous Testing and Feedback Loops: Spotify uses continuous integration and testing to ensure that each update meets the company's quality standards. Every feature goes through testing cycles that include unit tests, integration tests, and UX assessments to catch bugs early and align features with user expectations.

Real-Time User Feedback: Spotify constantly collects user feedback through in-app surveys and feature tests. This real-time feedback helps prioritize quality improvements that directly address user pain points and preferences, keeping the product user-centric.

This case shows how Spotify's agile approach enables the company to deliver frequent, high-quality updates while adapting quickly to market changes and user feedback.

Case Study 2: Atlassian – Agile Quality Management in Software Tools

Atlassian, the company behind popular software tools like Jira, Confluence, and Trello, utilizes agile quality management to maintain the quality and reliability of its products in a highly competitive software market.

Automated Testing and CI/CD: Atlassian uses an extensive suite of automated tests, including unit tests, integration tests, and regression tests, to maintain quality as new features and updates are added. CI/CD pipelines allow for frequent releases, ensuring that updates are delivered with minimal bugs and downtime.

Feature Flagging for Incremental Rollouts: Atlassian utilizes feature flags to deploy new features to a small subset of users first. This allows the team to gather feedback and monitor for issues on a smaller scale before rolling the feature out to a larger audience.

Collaborative Development and Quality Focus: Atlassian's agile development process includes regular cross-functional meetings where developers, product managers, and QA specialists collaborate to prioritize quality. They employ Scrum methodologies, with each sprint including dedicated testing phases that focus on quality improvements.

Through these practices, Atlassian ensures its products meet high standards of quality while being able to iterate quickly in response to customer needs and market demands.

Case Study 3: Google – Agile Quality Management for Web and Mobile Applications

Google employs agile quality management for many of its digital products, such as Google Maps and Google Photos, to maintain high standards of usability, performance, and reliability.

Rapid Prototyping and A/B Testing: Google uses rapid prototyping and A/B testing extensively to gather real-world user data before fully deploying new features. This agile approach allows Google to test multiple variations and select the best-performing option based on actual user feedback.

Focus on User-Centric Quality Metrics: Google's QA teams utilize user-centric quality metrics, such as load times, user retention rates, and error reports, to assess the quality of their products. This helps them ensure that updates not only meet functional requirements but also align with user expectations.

Cross-Functional Collaboration with Embedded QA: Google's development teams include embedded QA roles that work closely with developers throughout the development process. This integration allows for continuous testing and quality checks at every stage, from coding to deployment.

This case demonstrates how Google's agile quality management approach ensures its products consistently meet high standards and deliver a superior user experience.

Benefits of Agile Quality Management in Digital Product Development

Improved Responsiveness to User Needs: Agile quality management enables teams to incorporate user feedback throughout the development process, ensuring that the final product meets or exceeds user expectations.

Reduced Time to Market: By integrating quality checks and testing into every iteration, agile quality management reduces the time needed for final testing and bug fixing, speeding up the release of new features and updates.

Higher Product Quality: Continuous testing, real-time feedback, and collaboration across functions result in a higher standard of quality. This reduces the likelihood of post-release issues and enhances user satisfaction.

Enhanced Team Collaboration and Morale: Agile methodologies promote collaboration across departments, which can boost team morale and create a stronger shared focus on delivering a high-quality product.

Greater Flexibility and Adaptability: Agile quality management practices provide the flexibility to respond to changes in user preferences, technological advancements, or market demands. This is particularly valuable in fast-moving digital markets where agility is a competitive advantage.

Agile quality management is transforming how digital products are developed, enabling companies to maintain high standards while responding quickly to changing market demands and user expectations. Case studies from companies like Spotify, Atlassian, and Google highlight the effectiveness of agile methodologies in maintaining product quality, reducing development times, and aligning products with user needs.

As digital markets continue to evolve, agile quality management will likely become even more critical in enabling companies to deliver high-quality digital products efficiently. Through continuous testing, real-time feedback, collaboration, and iterative improvements, agile quality management offers a robust framework for quality that adapts to the fast-paced, user-focused nature of digital product development.

10. Building a Digital-First Quality Culture

10.1 Leadership in Digital Quality Management

In the digital age, leadership in quality management requires a transformative approach, prioritizing digital competencies, fostering an agile mindset, and cultivating a forward-thinking vision. With rapid technological advancements, leaders are challenged not only to uphold traditional quality standards but also to drive innovation and responsiveness, integrating cutting-edge tools and practices across their teams and processes. This section explores the essential role of leadership in navigating digital quality management, focusing on digital transformation strategies, fostering a culture of continuous improvement, and building adaptable quality teams.

The Evolving Role of Leadership in Quality Management

As quality management increasingly incorporates digital solutions, the traditional leadership role has expanded. Leaders must now guide their teams through complex digital landscapes, manage data-driven quality control, and ensure that technological adoption aligns with the organization's objectives. The role of a quality leader in the digital age encompasses:

Strategic Vision for Digital Transformation: Effective leaders establish a clear vision that defines how digital tools, such as AI, IoT, and big data analytics, will enhance quality processes. They drive alignment between digital initiatives and quality management goals, ensuring that investments in technology deliver measurable improvements.

Adaptability and Agility: Digital quality management requires agility to respond quickly to changing market conditions, technological advancements, and customer expectations. Leaders must foster an agile approach in quality processes, emphasizing flexibility and iterative improvements that allow teams to address issues proactively.

Cultivating a Data-Driven Culture: In a data-intensive environment, leaders are responsible for promoting a culture where data is central to decision-making. This involves training teams to interpret data insights, ensuring data quality, and using analytics to predict and mitigate quality risks.

Key Leadership Competencies in Digital Quality Management

To effectively lead digital quality initiatives, leaders need to develop a blend of technical, strategic, and interpersonal skills. Some critical competencies include:

Digital Literacy: Leaders must have a solid understanding of digital tools relevant to quality management, including quality management software (QMS), predictive analytics, and IoT-enabled systems. This technical knowledge allows them to make informed decisions about technology adoption and integration.

Change Management Expertise: Digital transformation in quality management can face resistance, as it often requires significant shifts in workflows and roles. Leaders need strong change management skills to communicate the benefits of digital adoption, manage transitions effectively, and support employees through the learning curve associated with new tools.

Visionary Thinking: Leaders must anticipate future trends in quality management, such as the integration of AI for defect detection or the use of blockchain for traceability. Visionary thinking enables them to strategically position the organization to leverage these technologies, maintaining a competitive edge in quality assurance.

Strategies for Leading Digital Quality Transformation

Leading digital quality transformation involves implementing specific strategies that align with organizational goals and the broader technological landscape. Here are key strategies leaders can employ:

Setting a Clear Digital Quality Roadmap

Developing a digital roadmap is essential for guiding the organization's quality transformation efforts. This roadmap outlines the digital tools, initiatives, and training required to achieve specific quality goals, helping align all stakeholders on priorities and timelines.

Empowering Cross-Functional Collaboration

Quality in the digital age often involves collaboration across multiple departments, including IT, production, and customer service. Leaders should encourage cross-functional collaboration, ensuring all departments contribute insights and align on shared quality objectives.

Investing in Employee Training and Development

As digital tools become central to quality processes, continuous learning is crucial. Leaders should facilitate training programs to enhance employees' digital skills, particularly in data analytics, predictive maintenance, and software use, empowering them to handle new tools confidently.

Promoting Real-Time Decision-Making and Responsiveness

Digital tools offer opportunities for real-time monitoring and swift decision-making. Leaders can establish real-time data access and reporting, enabling quality teams to respond to issues promptly and make data-driven adjustments that enhance efficiency.

Leveraging AI and Predictive Analytics for Proactive Quality Control

Digital transformation enables proactive approaches to quality management. Leaders can drive the adoption of predictive analytics to identify potential issues before they escalate, using insights from AI to optimize processes, reduce waste, and enhance product quality.

Building a Digital-Ready Quality Team

Creating a high-performing quality team capable of navigating digital tools and processes is central to effective leadership. To achieve this, leaders should focus on:

Hiring for Digital Competencies: When recruiting for quality roles, leaders should prioritize candidates with digital competencies, such as data analysis, familiarity with quality management software, and an understanding of emerging technologies relevant to quality.

Encouraging Data Literacy Across the Team: Data literacy enables quality teams to interpret and act on data insights effectively. Leaders should foster data literacy by organizing workshops, promoting knowledge-sharing sessions, and encouraging employees to use data-driven tools in daily tasks.

Creating a Culture of Innovation and Continuous Improvement: Leaders play a critical role in nurturing a culture where innovation is valued. This includes providing space for experimentation, rewarding creative problem-solving, and establishing processes for continuous feedback and iterative improvement.

Case Example: Leadership in Digital Quality Transformation

A prominent example of leadership in digital quality management can be seen in the automotive industry. Recognizing the impact of digital transformation on quality control, many automotive companies have implemented IoT-enabled sensors to monitor product quality in real time. Leaders in these companies adopted a phased approach, first piloting the technology, then gradually expanding its use across production lines, and finally training teams to interpret IoT data for predictive maintenance.

These leaders provided a structured roadmap for the digital transformation journey, aligning all stakeholders on key goals, such as reducing defect rates and improving customer satisfaction. By fostering cross-functional collaboration and investing in data analytics training, they successfully transformed quality management, ultimately leading to reduced recalls and enhanced product quality.

The Future of Leadership in Digital Quality Management

As digital transformation evolves, the role of leadership in quality management will continue to expand. Future trends include:

Increased Use of AI-Driven Quality Insights: Leaders will leverage AI-driven insights more extensively, making complex predictive analyses and automated quality control a routine part of quality management.

Focus on Cybersecurity and Data Privacy: With the rise in digital data collection, cybersecurity and data privacy will become critical areas of focus. Leaders must prioritize strategies to protect data integrity and maintain customer trust.

Integration of Digital Twins: As digital twin technology becomes more common, leaders will explore its applications in quality control, using real-time digital replicas of products and processes to identify potential defects and optimize quality.

Leadership in digital quality management is pivotal for successfully navigating the complexities of digital transformation. By setting a clear vision, fostering a data-driven culture, and empowering teams with the skills and tools needed, leaders can drive quality improvements that meet modern standards and exceed customer expectations. The transformative power of digital quality management is vast, but realizing its potential requires leaders who are adaptable, visionary, and committed to continuous innovation. As organizations continue to adapt to a digital landscape, effective leadership will remain a cornerstone of success in quality management.

10.2 Developing Skills and Capabilities for Digital Quality

In an era where digital transformation is reshaping industries, the quality management function within organizations must evolve to keep pace. Traditional skills in quality control and assurance are no longer sufficient; quality teams now require a blend of technical, analytical, and digital skills to manage the complexities of digital quality. This shift demands a redefined skill set, where data analytics, automation proficiency, and cross-functional communication become pivotal in achieving digital quality objectives.

This section explores the essential skills and capabilities for a quality team focused on digital quality, emphasizing the importance of training, development, and adaptation in the digital age.

1. Key Skills for a Digitally Focused Quality Team

To thrive in a digital landscape, quality teams must be equipped with a diverse set of skills that go beyond traditional quality assurance. Below are some of the critical skills and capabilities necessary for digital quality management.

1.1 Data Analytics and Interpretation

Why It's Important: As data-driven decision-making becomes central to quality management, quality professionals must be skilled in collecting, analyzing, and interpreting data. This enables them to identify patterns, detect anomalies, and predict potential quality issues.

Key Competencies:

Data Visualization: The ability to visualize data using tools like Power BI, Tableau, or Google Data Studio is essential for communicating insights to non-technical stakeholders effectively.

Statistical Analysis: Proficiency in statistical methods, such as regression analysis, correlation, and hypothesis testing, enables teams to draw meaningful insights from complex datasets.

Root Cause Analysis: Skills in root cause analysis are essential for identifying underlying quality issues. Techniques such as the 5 Whys and Fishbone Diagram can be enhanced by digital tools to provide faster and more accurate insights.

Tools and Technologies: R, Python, SQL, Minitab, and advanced Excel.

1.2 Proficiency in Digital Quality Management Systems (QMS)

Why It's Important: Digital QMS platforms are central to modern quality management, as they streamline processes, automate workflows, and provide a centralized repository for quality data. Familiarity with these systems enhances the efficiency and reliability of quality functions.

Key Competencies:

System Navigation and Data Entry: Basic proficiency in navigating QMS platforms, entering data accurately, and using built-in analytical tools.

Configuration and Customization: Advanced users benefit from understanding how to configure QMS settings to align with specific organizational needs.

Workflow Automation: Automating routine tasks, such as compliance tracking and reporting, reduces manual work and minimizes the potential for human error.

Tools and Technologies: Quality management software like MasterControl, Sparta TrackWise, and Intelex.

1.3 Understanding of IoT and Smart Sensors

Why It's Important: Internet of Things (IoT) technology and smart sensors play a vital role in real-time quality monitoring. Quality professionals need to understand how these devices work and how to use the data they generate to inform decision-making.

Key Competencies:

IoT Device Management: Understanding IoT device capabilities and limitations, including calibration and maintenance of sensors.

Real-Time Data Monitoring: The ability to interpret data from smart sensors and IoT devices to monitor quality conditions in real time.

Integration with QMS: Skills in integrating IoT data with digital QMS systems to facilitate seamless data flow and automated quality tracking.

Tools and Technologies: IoT platforms such as AWS IoT Core, Azure IoT Hub, and custom IoT devices used for quality control.

1.4 Knowledge of Artificial Intelligence (AI) and Machine Learning (ML)

Why It's Important: AI and ML have emerged as powerful tools in quality management, enabling predictive analytics, anomaly detection, and process optimization. Quality professionals should understand AI and ML concepts to leverage these tools effectively.

Key Competencies:

Predictive Analytics: Understanding how to use predictive models to forecast potential quality issues before they occur.

Anomaly Detection: AI can detect outliers in production data, allowing quality teams to intervene proactively.

Process Optimization: ML algorithms can be used to analyze production processes and suggest improvements based on historical data.

Tools and Technologies: TensorFlow, Scikit-Learn, and specialized AI/ML platforms integrated with QMS.

1.5 Cybersecurity Awareness

Why It's Important: As digital quality management relies heavily on data, cybersecurity becomes crucial in protecting sensitive quality information and maintaining data integrity.

Key Competencies:

Data Protection: Understanding the basics of data encryption, data masking, and access controls.

Incident Response: Familiarity with protocols for responding to cybersecurity incidents, including reporting, containment, and resolution.

Compliance: Knowledge of regulatory standards such as GDPR, CCPA, and industry-specific cybersecurity requirements.

Tools and Technologies: Security tools like firewalls, antivirus software, and enterprise cybersecurity platforms.

1.6 Agile Methodologies

Why It's Important: Agile methodologies foster a culture of continuous improvement and flexibility, which is essential for digital quality management in fast-paced environments. Teams need to adapt quickly to changing requirements and customer expectations.

Key Competencies:

Sprint Planning and Management: Skills in planning and managing sprints to ensure continuous progress and adaptability.

Scrum Framework: Familiarity with the Scrum framework, including roles like Scrum Master, Product Owner, and practices like daily stand-ups and retrospectives.

Iterative Development: Emphasis on incremental improvements that allow for regular quality assessments and adjustments.

Tools and Technologies: Jira, Trello, and other agile project management tools.

1.7 Cross-Functional Communication and Collaboration

Why It's Important: Digital quality management often requires close collaboration with IT, data science, production, and customer service teams. Communication skills are crucial for ensuring alignment across departments.

Key Competencies:

Effective Communication: Ability to convey technical information to non-technical stakeholders and vice versa.

Collaboration: Skills in working within cross-functional teams to integrate quality management objectives with other departmental goals.

Feedback and Adaptability: Openness to feedback from multiple sources and adaptability to changing project scopes.

Tools and Technologies: Slack, Microsoft Teams, and collaborative project management software.

2. Training and Development for Building Digital Quality Capabilities

Developing a digitally skilled quality team requires targeted training and continuous development programs. Companies can build effective development strategies by focusing on the following approaches:

2.1 On-the-Job Training and Mentorship

On-the-Job Training: Practical experience is invaluable, particularly with emerging digital tools and methodologies. On-the-job training allows employees to learn in real-time, applying their new skills directly to their responsibilities.

Mentorship Programs: Pairing less experienced team members with senior quality professionals who have expertise in digital tools can accelerate learning and foster a supportive learning environment.

2.2 Certification Programs and Courses

Digital Quality Certifications: Certifications like Certified Quality Engineer (CQE) or Six Sigma Green Belt, with a focus on digital quality, are valuable in building credibility and knowledge in digital quality management.

Courses on Data Science and Analytics: Courses in data science, machine learning, and AI provide quality teams with the analytical skills necessary for modern quality management.

2.3 Encouraging a Culture of Continuous Learning

Incentives for Skill Development: Providing incentives for completing relevant courses or certifications can encourage team members to continuously upgrade their skills.

Learning Management Systems (LMS): An LMS can host a range of digital quality management resources, providing easy access to training materials, tutorials, and industry case studies.

Building a digitally focused quality team is an ongoing process that requires strategic investment in skill development. By equipping quality professionals with data analytics, IoT knowledge, AI and ML capabilities, cybersecurity awareness, agile methodologies, and cross-functional communication skills, organizations can ensure that their quality teams are ready to meet the demands of digital transformation.

In the dynamic landscape of digital quality, training and development play a critical role in helping quality teams stay ahead of technological advances and continuously improve their capabilities.

10.3 Encouraging Innovation and Continuous Improvement in Digital Quality Management

In today's rapidly evolving digital landscape, fostering a culture of innovation and continuous improvement is essential for organizations to stay competitive and responsive to market demands. Digital transformation in quality management not only requires adapting to new technologies but also embracing a mindset that encourages innovation, agility, and proactive problem-solving.

This section explores the importance of nurturing a culture of innovation, best practices for driving continuous improvement in quality processes, and ways to adapt to the ever-changing technological environment.

1. Importance of Fostering a Culture of Innovation and Adaptation

A culture of innovation enables organizations to continuously explore new ideas, tools, and strategies for improvement. In quality management, innovation can lead to more effective processes, better products, and increased customer satisfaction. The ability to innovate is especially critical in the digital age, where technology and customer expectations are constantly shifting.

1.1 Benefits of Innovation in Quality Management

Enhanced Process Efficiency: Innovation leads to improved processes that reduce waste, optimize resources, and increase efficiency.

Proactive Problem-Solving: Encouraging innovation allows teams to identify potential issues early and develop creative solutions.

Improved Customer Satisfaction: By continually improving quality processes, organizations can better meet or exceed customer expectations, creating loyal customers.

Adaptability to Market Changes: Innovative organizations are better equipped to adapt to shifts in market conditions, regulatory changes, and technological advancements.

1.2 Characteristics of a Culture of Innovation

Openness to Experimentation: Teams feel encouraged to experiment with new ideas without fear of failure.

Collaborative Environment: Cross-functional collaboration is prioritized to ensure diverse perspectives contribute to problem-solving.

Continuous Learning: A commitment to continuous learning ensures that employees have the latest knowledge and skills to support innovation.

Recognition and Reward: Recognizing and rewarding innovative efforts helps motivate team members to actively contribute to a culture of improvement.

2. Driving Continuous Improvement in Quality Processes

Continuous improvement (CI) is a systematic approach to enhancing processes, products, and services incrementally over time. In quality management, CI can be achieved through a range of digital tools and methodologies that support data-driven decision-making and automation.

2.1 Key Continuous Improvement Techniques

2.1.1 Plan-Do-Check-Act (PDCA)

The PDCA cycle, developed by W. Edwards Deming, is a cornerstone of continuous improvement. Each stage promotes structured problem-solving and systematic experimentation:

Plan: Identify an area for improvement, set objectives, and plan the changes needed.

Do: Implement the changes on a small scale to test their impact.

Check: Analyze the results to determine if the changes achieved the desired outcome.

Act: If successful, implement the changes on a broader scale. If not, refine and repeat the cycle.

2.1.2 Lean and Six Sigma

Lean and Six Sigma methodologies focus on reducing waste and improving quality through data-driven decision-making. These methods involve specific tools, such as value stream mapping, root cause analysis, and DMAIC (Define, Measure, Analyze, Improve, Control), which support quality teams in eliminating inefficiencies and enhancing process reliability.

2.1.3 Kaizen

Kaizen, a Japanese term for "continuous improvement," involves small, incremental changes made by employees at all levels. Kaizen empowers employees to contribute ideas for improvements and ensures that every member of the team plays a role in enhancing quality.

2.1.4 Agile Methodologies

Adopting agile methodologies in quality management fosters flexibility, responsiveness, and rapid iteration. Agile encourages frequent feedback loops, iterative improvements, and collaboration across teams. Agile quality management allows for adaptability and quicker response times to quality issues.

2.2 Implementing Continuous Improvement Through Digital Tools

Digital tools streamline continuous improvement efforts by automating data collection, analysis, and reporting, enabling real-time quality monitoring and providing actionable insights for improvement.

Data Analytics Platforms: Tools like Power BI, Tableau, and custom dashboards enable real-time data analysis, allowing quality teams to identify improvement opportunities quickly.

Digital QMS: Quality Management Systems (QMS) automate compliance tracking, quality audits, and documentation, simplifying the process of continuous quality improvement.

Collaborative Platforms: Digital collaboration tools like Microsoft Teams and Slack enable cross-functional communication, ensuring that all relevant stakeholders are involved in improvement efforts.

3. Encouraging a Mindset of Adaptation and Agility

Digital transformation requires a mindset that embraces change, adapts to new challenges, and seeks innovative solutions. To build such a mindset, organizations need to create an environment where employees feel empowered to experiment, learn from failure, and share ideas.

3.1 Building a Resilient Workforce

Building resilience within teams allows them to adapt to new technologies and processes effectively. This involves training, development, and empowerment.

Training for Agility: Providing training on digital tools, change management, and problem-solving skills prepares employees to handle dynamic challenges.

Empowering Decision-Making: Empowering employees to make decisions within their areas of expertise fosters a sense of ownership, encouraging proactive problem-solving and adaptation.

3.2 Rewarding Innovation and Improvement Efforts

Recognition and rewards can motivate employees to contribute ideas and improvements. When team members see that their efforts toward innovation and quality improvement are valued, they are more likely to stay engaged and continue contributing to a culture of improvement.

Incentive Programs: Create incentive programs that reward employees who propose and implement successful quality improvements.

Recognition: Publicly recognizing team members for their innovative contributions builds morale and fosters a positive work culture.

3.3 Creating Feedback Loops for Improvement

Establishing structured feedback mechanisms ensures that quality processes are constantly evaluated and refined. Feedback can come from internal teams, customers, or suppliers.

Internal Feedback: Regular team meetings and review sessions help identify areas for improvement in quality processes.

Customer Feedback: Integrating customer feedback through surveys, social media, or direct communication enables teams to understand customer expectations and areas for improvement.

Supplier Collaboration: Working closely with suppliers and obtaining their feedback on quality standards can enhance quality across the supply chain.

4. Tools and Technologies Supporting Innovation and Continuous Improvement

In a digital environment, leveraging technology to drive innovation and continuous improvement in quality management is essential. Several digital tools support innovation efforts by facilitating collaboration, real-time data analysis, and automation.

4.1 Digital Collaboration Platforms

Digital collaboration tools like Microsoft Teams, Slack, and Trello enable cross-functional communication and real-time project tracking. These tools are essential for fostering a collaborative environment where quality teams can share ideas, provide feedback, and work together on improvement initiatives.

4.2 Real-Time Data Analytics Tools

Data analytics platforms, such as Tableau, Power BI, and Google Data Studio, allow quality teams to analyze data in real time, identify patterns, and make data-driven decisions. Real-time data analysis supports proactive quality management and allows for rapid response to emerging quality issues.

4.3 Automation Software

Automation tools streamline repetitive tasks, such as data entry, reporting, and compliance tracking, freeing up team members to focus on higher-value activities. Automated workflows improve process efficiency and reduce the potential for human error in quality processes.

4.4 Knowledge Management Systems

Knowledge management systems store and organize institutional knowledge, enabling employees to access valuable information on quality standards, best practices, and previous improvement efforts. By making this information easily accessible, knowledge management systems encourage continuous learning and improvement across the organization.

Encouraging innovation and continuous improvement is essential for maintaining high standards of quality in a rapidly changing digital world. By fostering a culture of innovation, investing in digital tools, and adopting agile methodologies, organizations can drive continuous improvements in their quality management processes. Equipping quality teams with the right skills, resources, and support to experiment, learn, and adapt enables them to meet customer expectations, respond to new challenges, and achieve long-term success in digital quality management.

11. Risk Management and Compliance in the Digital Age

11.1 Identifying New Risks in Digital Quality Management

In the digital era, quality management faces a spectrum of new risks driven by advancements in technology, increasing reliance on data, and a constantly evolving regulatory landscape. While digital tools and solutions have transformed quality management by enabling real-time data analysis, automation, and predictive insights, they also introduce unique vulnerabilities that can impact organizational performance and customer trust.

This section examines key risks in digital quality management, focusing on cybersecurity threats, data privacy issues, and operational risks, all of which need proactive identification and mitigation to maintain a resilient quality framework.

1. Cybersecurity Risks in Digital Quality Management

As quality management systems become more digital, cybersecurity risks have become increasingly significant. Digital QMS platforms, Internet of Things (IoT) devices, and cloud storage solutions are commonly used in quality management but also create vulnerabilities that malicious actors can exploit.

1.1 Threats Posed by Cybersecurity Risks

1.1.1 Unauthorized Access

Cybercriminals may attempt to gain unauthorized access to sensitive quality data, including customer information, quality test results, and compliance documentation. If successful, this can lead to data breaches, loss of confidential information, and damage to brand reputation.

1.1.2 Malware and Ransomware

Quality management systems and digital tools can be targeted by malware and ransomware attacks, leading to data corruption, downtime, and costly recovery processes. Ransomware attacks may freeze access to critical quality data, disrupting operational workflows.

1.1.3 Phishing and Social Engineering

Employees in quality management are often targeted through phishing emails and social engineering tactics, aiming to trick them into providing access credentials or downloading malicious software. Phishing attacks can undermine the security of digital quality management systems and jeopardize data integrity.

1.2 Mitigating Cybersecurity Risks

1.2.1 Implementing Strong Access Controls

Access controls ensure that only authorized personnel have access to sensitive quality data. Implementing role-based access and using multi-factor authentication (MFA) are effective ways to limit unauthorized access.

1.2.2 Regular Security Audits

Conducting regular security audits helps identify and address potential vulnerabilities in digital quality systems. Audits can uncover gaps in cybersecurity protocols, allowing organizations to reinforce defenses before they are exploited.

1.2.3 Cybersecurity Training

Training quality management teams on cybersecurity best practices helps prevent phishing and other attacks. Awareness programs equip employees with the skills to recognize threats and avoid risky behaviors that could compromise system security.

2. Data Privacy Risks

With digital quality management heavily reliant on data collection and analysis, organizations must address data privacy concerns to comply with legal requirements and maintain customer trust. Data privacy risks involve unauthorized use, exposure, or mismanagement of sensitive data, which can lead to regulatory penalties and reputational damage.

2.1 Common Data Privacy Concerns

2.1.1 Handling Personally Identifiable Information (PII)

Many quality management processes involve handling customer or employee data, which may include PII. Mishandling or exposing this data can lead to regulatory violations and damage customer relationships.

2.1.2 Data Storage and Transfer

Data stored in cloud systems or transferred across digital platforms can be exposed to privacy risks. Ensuring secure data storage and encrypted data transfer are essential to maintaining data privacy.

2.1.3 Compliance with Data Protection Regulations

Organizations must comply with data privacy laws like the General Data Protection Regulation (GDPR) and the California Consumer

Privacy Act (CCPA). Non-compliance can result in legal penalties and impact customer trust.

2.2 Strategies for Mitigating Data Privacy Risks

2.2.1 Implementing Data Encryption

Encryption protects data by making it unreadable to unauthorized users. Encrypting sensitive data both at rest and in transit minimizes the risk of exposure if data is intercepted.

2.2.2 Anonymizing Sensitive Data

Anonymization removes identifiable information from data sets, allowing quality teams to use the data for analysis without risking privacy breaches. This technique is valuable for maintaining data utility while protecting privacy.

2.2.3 Regular Data Privacy Audits

Regular audits ensure that data management practices comply with privacy regulations and internal standards. Audits can identify privacy risks, such as outdated protocols, unprotected files, or inappropriate access permissions.

3. Operational Risks in Digital Quality Management

Operational risks in digital quality management include risks associated with system outages, technology failure, and process inconsistencies. These risks can disrupt quality processes and impact an organization's ability to deliver reliable products and services.

3.1 Common Operational Risks

3.1.1 System Downtime

Digital quality management systems rely on uninterrupted access to data and software applications. System outages due to hardware failures, software issues, or network disruptions can hinder quality processes and delay production.

3.1.2 Technology Integration Challenges

Integrating various digital tools, such as Quality Management Systems (QMS), Enterprise Resource Planning (ERP) software, and IoT devices, can be complex. Misalignment between these systems can result in data inconsistencies and workflow disruptions.

3.1.3 Lack of Skilled Workforce

The shift toward digital quality management requires employees with technical skills in data analytics, cybersecurity, and digital quality tools. A lack of skilled personnel can lead to inefficient use of digital resources and increase operational risks.

3.2 Mitigating Operational Risks

3.2.1 Implementing Redundant Systems

Redundant systems provide a backup in case of a primary system failure. For example, implementing redundant data storage solutions ensures that critical quality data remains accessible during system outages.

3.2.2 Cross-Training Employees

Cross-training helps build a flexible workforce capable of handling various digital quality management tasks. Employees trained in multiple roles can cover for one another in case of unexpected absences or skill gaps.

3.2.3 Continuous System Monitoring

Monitoring digital systems in real time allows quality teams to detect and respond to system issues before they escalate. Automated monitoring tools provide alerts for potential problems, helping teams maintain consistent quality operations.

Identifying and addressing the new risks associated with digital quality management is critical for maintaining effective and reliable quality processes. Cybersecurity, data privacy, and operational risks pose unique challenges, requiring proactive mitigation strategies such as implementing robust access controls, encrypting data, and developing a skilled workforce. By understanding and managing these risks, organizations can enhance the resilience and effectiveness of their digital quality management practices, ensuring continuous improvement in product and service quality while safeguarding stakeholder trust.

11.2 Ensuring Compliance with Digital Quality Standards

In an increasingly digital landscape, adherence to established quality standards and regulatory compliance is crucial for companies to maintain competitive advantage and uphold customer trust. Digital quality standards, including ISO 9001 for quality management systems and ISO 27001 for information security, offer frameworks that guide organizations in establishing effective processes, maintaining data security, and achieving consistent quality outputs. As digital quality management involves the use of advanced technologies, interconnected systems, and extensive data, meeting these standards requires a structured approach that incorporates digital-specific practices, tools, and compliance strategies.

This section explores the importance of compliance with digital quality standards, highlights relevant standards for quality and data security, and discusses key practices organizations can adopt to ensure compliance in the digital age.

1. The Importance of Compliance in Digital Quality Management

As organizations digitize quality processes, compliance with standards is essential for ensuring the reliability, security, and efficiency of digital quality management. Compliance helps organizations mitigate risks, reduce operational inefficiencies, and maintain quality consistency across digital platforms.

1.1 Building Trust with Customers and Stakeholders

Standards like ISO 9001 and ISO 27001 are internationally recognized and provide assurance to customers, stakeholders, and partners that an organization adheres to rigorous quality and security practices. Compliance demonstrates a commitment to high standards of performance, which enhances trust and strengthens business relationships.

1.2 Reducing Risk of Operational Disruptions

Compliance with digital quality standards helps organizations establish a framework for identifying, evaluating, and mitigating risks. Standards for information security, such as ISO 27001, protect digital assets and prevent data breaches that can disrupt operations. In addition, compliance with quality management standards minimizes the likelihood of process breakdowns and quality failures.

1.3 Meeting Regulatory Requirements

Many industries, including healthcare, finance, and manufacturing, have specific regulatory requirements that overlap with quality standards. Ensuring compliance with standards like ISO 9001 helps organizations align their practices with regulatory expectations, reducing the risk of penalties, legal issues, and reputational damage.

2. Key Digital Quality Standards

Digital quality management requires adherence to standards that address quality assurance, data security, and process consistency. Below are some key standards that organizations in the digital age should consider implementing:

2.1 ISO 9001: Quality Management Systems

ISO 9001 is a globally recognized standard for quality management systems (QMS) that emphasizes process efficiency, customer satisfaction, and continuous improvement. For organizations using digital quality tools, ISO 9001 provides a structured approach to establishing consistent quality practices.

Key Elements of ISO 9001:

Process Approach: Encourages organizations to understand and optimize interrelated processes for improved efficiency.

Customer Focus: Promotes practices that prioritize customer needs and expectations.

Continuous Improvement: Emphasizes regular assessment and refinement of processes to maintain high-quality outputs.

2.2 ISO 27001: Information Security Management Systems

ISO 27001 focuses on information security management, helping organizations protect sensitive data from cyber threats, unauthorized access, and breaches. As digital quality management involves extensive data use, ISO 27001 is critical for securing quality-related information.

Key Elements of ISO 27001:

Risk Assessment: Identifying potential risks to information security and implementing measures to mitigate them.

Access Control: Limiting access to sensitive data based on user roles and responsibilities.

Incident Response: Developing a framework for responding to and recovering from security incidents.

2.3 Other Relevant Standards

ISO 22301 (Business Continuity): Ensures that organizations can continue operations in the event of disruptions, supporting resilience in digital quality management.

GDPR Compliance (for EU-based companies): Ensures data privacy and protection, particularly when handling customer data in quality processes.

ISO 31000 (Risk Management): Provides a framework for identifying, assessing, and managing risks, which is essential for organizations navigating digital quality transformation.

3. Steps to Ensure Compliance with Digital Quality Standards

Achieving and maintaining compliance with digital quality standards requires a structured approach. The following steps can help organizations establish robust compliance processes that support quality management in the digital age:

3.1 Conducting a Compliance Assessment

An initial compliance assessment provides insights into the organization's current state concerning digital quality standards. The assessment should evaluate quality management practices, data security measures, and risk management frameworks to identify gaps that need addressing.

Steps for a Compliance Assessment:

Gap Analysis: Identify areas where current practices fall short of standard requirements.

Risk Evaluation: Assess potential risks associated with non-compliance, such as data breaches or process inefficiencies.

Prioritization: Rank areas that require immediate attention, focusing on high-risk gaps first.

3.2 Implementing Digital Quality Management Software (QMS)

Digital QMS platforms streamline compliance by providing tools for process documentation, audit tracking, and data management. Many digital QMS systems come equipped with features that facilitate ISO compliance by automating documentation, workflow approvals, and quality monitoring.

Benefits of Digital QMS:

Real-Time Monitoring: Enables continuous tracking of quality metrics and process performance.

Automated Documentation: Ensures compliance documentation is updated, organized, and easily accessible for audits.

Audit Trail: Digital QMS platforms create an audit trail that documents all actions, changes, and reviews within the system, making it easier to demonstrate compliance.

3.3 Training Employees on Compliance Requirements

Employee training is essential for embedding compliance into the organization's culture. Quality and security teams, as well as employees who handle quality data, should receive training on standards such as ISO 9001 and ISO 27001.

Key Training Areas:

Understanding Standards: Educating teams on the principles and requirements of ISO standards.

Data Security Best Practices: Ensuring employees understand cybersecurity protocols, such as secure data handling and recognizing phishing threats.

Compliance-Related Roles: Clarifying employee responsibilities concerning compliance tasks, such as documentation and reporting.

3.4 Conducting Regular Internal Audits

Internal audits help organizations monitor compliance and address any deviations from quality standards. Audits provide an opportunity to identify improvement areas, ensure corrective actions are effective, and prepare the organization for external audits.

Steps for Conducting an Internal Audit:

Plan the Audit: Define audit objectives, scope, and the processes to be reviewed.

Gather Evidence: Review quality records, data logs, and security documentation to evaluate compliance.

Identify Non-Conformities: Document instances where processes do not meet standard requirements.

Implement Corrective Actions: Develop and implement a corrective action plan to address non-conformities.

3.5 Leveraging Automation for Compliance

Automation is increasingly essential for managing compliance in digital quality management. Automated solutions can streamline repetitive compliance tasks, such as data entry, reporting, and documentation, which reduces human error and enhances process efficiency.

Examples of Automation in Compliance:

Automated Reporting: Automatically generates compliance reports that can be shared with quality teams and auditors.

Alert Systems: Notifies teams of compliance deviations or upcoming audit requirements.

Continuous Monitoring: Uses sensors, software, and IoT devices to monitor quality metrics in real time, ensuring that processes remain compliant.

Ensuring compliance with digital quality standards is fundamental for effective quality management in the digital age. By adhering to standards such as ISO 9001 and ISO 27001, organizations can build trust with stakeholders, reduce risks, and maintain consistent quality across digital platforms. Implementing digital QMS software, conducting regular audits, and training employees are essential steps toward maintaining a compliant and resilient quality management framework. Embracing automation and continuous monitoring can further enhance compliance efforts, allowing organizations to adapt to evolving standards and regulatory requirements while achieving digital quality excellence.

11.3 Building a Resilient Quality Management System

In today's digital landscape, building a resilient Quality Management System (QMS) is essential for organizations to withstand disruptions and adapt to changing market demands. A resilient QMS emphasizes risk mitigation, robustness, and flexibility, ensuring that quality processes remain effective under a variety of conditions. As digital transformation accelerates, quality management systems must be fortified to address new challenges like cybersecurity threats, data privacy concerns, and technological advancements. This section explores key strategies for enhancing the resilience of QMS through proactive risk mitigation, structural robustness, and adaptability to changing environments.

1. Understanding Resilience in Quality Management

Resilience in a QMS refers to its ability to maintain stable and high-quality outputs despite disruptions, uncertainties, or changes in the operating environment. A resilient QMS not only helps prevent quality issues but also enables organizations to recover quickly from unexpected challenges. Unlike traditional QMS, which may focus primarily on maintaining standards, a resilient QMS emphasizes continuous adaptation, learning, and improvement.

1.1 The Importance of Resilience in a Digital Environment

In a digital environment, resilience is critical due to increased interconnectivity and dependence on technology. Digital QMS systems, which rely on software and data, face unique risks, including cyber threats, system failures, and data breaches. Moreover, rapid market shifts and regulatory changes necessitate a flexible approach to quality management.

1.2 Key Elements of a Resilient QMS

To build resilience, a QMS should focus on several key elements:

Proactive Risk Management: Identifying, assessing, and addressing potential risks before they impact quality.

Redundancy and Fail-Safes: Implementing backup systems and processes to maintain continuity.

Data-Driven Decision-Making: Using analytics to monitor quality metrics and detect early signs of issues.

Continuous Improvement: Regularly assessing and updating processes to stay aligned with industry standards and emerging challenges.

2. Strategies for Building a Resilient Quality Management System

Building a resilient QMS involves strategic actions at multiple levels, from risk assessment and mitigation to incorporating adaptable technology. Below are some core strategies that organizations can implement to enhance resilience in their quality management systems.

2.1 Conducting Comprehensive Risk Assessments

A comprehensive risk assessment is the foundation of a resilient QMS. By identifying vulnerabilities and potential risks, organizations can implement targeted mitigation strategies to protect against disruptions. Risk assessments should cover operational, technological, and compliance-related risks.

Steps for Effective Risk Assessment:

Identify Potential Risks: List risks specific to quality management, including cyber threats, supplier inconsistencies, and equipment failures.

Assess Likelihood and Impact: Determine the probability and potential impact of each risk on the QMS.

Develop Mitigation Strategies: Prioritize high-risk areas and create action plans to minimize their likelihood or impact.

Monitor and Reassess: Regularly review and update the risk assessment to reflect new threats and vulnerabilities.

2.2 Establishing Robust Cybersecurity Measures

As quality management becomes more digital, safeguarding data and systems from cyber threats is crucial. Implementing strong cybersecurity measures ensures that quality processes are not compromised by unauthorized access, data tampering, or system downtime.

Key Cybersecurity Measures for QMS Resilience:

Access Control: Limit access to quality data and QMS software to authorized personnel only.

Data Encryption: Use encryption to protect sensitive information within the QMS, especially during data transmission.

Regular Security Audits: Conduct routine security assessments to identify potential vulnerabilities and address them proactively.

Incident Response Plan: Develop a response plan for cybersecurity incidents to minimize impact on quality processes and facilitate quick recovery.

2.3 Leveraging Redundancy and Backup Systems

To ensure continuity in quality management, organizations should implement redundancy and backup systems for critical processes. Redundancy minimizes the impact of system failures or disruptions by allowing operations to continue uninterrupted.

Examples of Redundancy in QMS:

Data Backup: Store backup copies of quality data on secure, offsite servers to prevent data loss in case of a system failure.

Redundant Equipment: Have backup equipment for critical quality control tools, such as testing and inspection devices.

Automated Alerts: Set up automated notifications to alert teams about potential failures or performance deviations, allowing for timely interventions.

2.4 Embracing Flexibility and Agility in Processes

In a dynamic environment, flexibility and agility are essential components of resilience. A resilient QMS should have adaptable processes that allow for quick adjustments in response to market or operational changes.

Steps for Building Flexibility:

Modular Process Design: Create modular processes that can be easily modified or replaced without disrupting the entire system.

Cross-Training Employees: Train staff in multiple quality management roles so they can quickly adapt to different tasks as needed.

Regular Process Reviews: Continuously assess and update quality processes to ensure they align with evolving industry standards and best practices.

2.5 Implementing Data Analytics for Proactive Quality Management

Data analytics plays a crucial role in identifying early signs of quality issues, enabling organizations to take preventive actions. By leveraging data from various quality metrics, organizations can detect trends, anticipate potential disruptions, and make informed decisions.

Benefits of Data Analytics in QMS Resilience:

Early Detection: Identify potential problems before they affect product quality.

Predictive Maintenance: Use analytics to forecast equipment maintenance needs, reducing downtime and extending asset life.

Root Cause Analysis: Analyze data to understand the underlying causes of recurring issues and implement corrective measures.

3. Building a Culture of Resilience in Quality Management

While strategies and tools are essential, creating a culture that values resilience is equally important. A resilient culture empowers employees to proactively address quality issues, adapt to changes, and continuously improve quality management practices.

3.1 Promoting Employee Engagement and Empowerment

Employees play a crucial role in maintaining a resilient QMS. Engaging and empowering staff encourages them to take ownership of quality processes, identify potential issues early, and suggest improvements.

Actions for Fostering Engagement:

Provide Training: Offer regular training on risk management, cybersecurity, and quality standards.

Encourage Open Communication: Establish channels for employees to report quality concerns or suggest process improvements.

Recognize Contributions: Acknowledge and reward employees who demonstrate a proactive approach to quality resilience.

3.2 Encouraging Continuous Learning and Improvement

Continuous learning is a fundamental aspect of resilience. By fostering a culture that values learning, organizations ensure that their QMS remains agile and capable of addressing new challenges.

Steps to Promote Continuous Learning:

Regular Training Programs: Offer ongoing training on emerging technologies, industry standards, and best practices.

Internal Knowledge Sharing: Facilitate knowledge sharing among teams to enhance collective expertise in quality management.

Innovation Incentives: Encourage employees to experiment with new approaches and reward successful innovations in quality management.

Building a resilient Quality Management System is essential for organizations to navigate the complexities of a digital environment and maintain high standards of quality. By conducting thorough risk assessments, implementing strong cybersecurity measures, and embracing flexibility in processes, organizations can build a QMS capable of withstanding disruptions and adapting to changes. Leveraging data analytics further strengthens resilience, enabling proactive decision-making and early identification of potential quality issues.

Cultivating a culture of resilience within the organization, through employee engagement and continuous learning, ensures that all team members contribute to maintaining and enhancing the quality management system. As organizations continue their digital transformation journey, a resilient QMS will be a critical asset, supporting both operational stability and sustained quality excellence.

12. Case Studies: Digital Transformation Success Stories
12.1 Case Study 1: Manufacturing Industry

12.1 Case Study 1: Manufacturing Industry

How Digital Tools Improved Quality Processes in a Leading Manufacturing Company

Digital transformation is reshaping the manufacturing industry, driving significant improvements in quality management processes. In this case study, we'll explore how a major manufacturing company implemented digital tools to streamline its quality processes, resulting in improved accuracy, efficiency, and customer satisfaction. This case study highlights the challenges the company faced, the digital solutions they implemented, and the resulting benefits.

Background: Company Profile and Initial Challenges

Company Profile:

The company in focus is a global leader in the automotive manufacturing industry, known for its extensive production of vehicle components. With a network of factories and suppliers spread across multiple countries, the company produces high-precision parts used by major car manufacturers worldwide.

Initial Challenges:

Before digital transformation, the company struggled with several issues in its quality management processes:

Inconsistent Quality Standards: With multiple production facilities, maintaining consistent quality across locations was challenging. Quality standards varied, leading to inconsistencies in product quality.

Limited Data Integration: Quality data from different plants were recorded manually or stored in siloed systems. As a result, the company faced delays in data retrieval and analysis.

Inefficiencies in Defect Detection: Manual inspection processes were prone to human error, causing delays in identifying defects and responding to issues.

Supplier Quality Control Issues: The company's reliance on a large supplier network made it difficult to monitor supplier quality effectively and in real-time.

These challenges impacted not only production efficiency but also the company's reputation, as variations in quality led to occasional customer complaints and recalls. Recognizing the need for improvement, the company embarked on a digital transformation initiative focused on quality management.

Digital Transformation Initiative

The company's digital transformation in quality management centered around the adoption of advanced technologies, including artificial intelligence (AI), machine learning (ML), Internet of Things (IoT), and real-time data analytics. The goal was to create a more integrated, automated, and data-driven quality management system.

1. Implementing a Quality Management System (QMS) with Real-Time Data Analytics

The company began by deploying a centralized Quality Management System (QMS) that integrated data from all production facilities. This QMS was connected to a real-time data analytics platform, allowing for consistent data collection and analysis across locations. The platform aggregated quality data from various production lines, enabling the company to monitor quality metrics in real-time and identify trends or anomalies.

Key Features of the QMS:

Data Integration: Combined data from sensors, production machines, and inspection tools in real-time.

Automated Reporting: Generated instant reports on quality metrics, reducing the time and effort needed for manual reporting.

Customizable Dashboards: Provided quality engineers with tailored dashboards to monitor critical metrics relevant to each facility.

The integrated QMS allowed for faster identification of quality issues, enabling proactive corrective actions. By standardizing data across production sites, the company achieved greater consistency in quality standards.

2. IoT-Enabled Smart Sensors for Defect Detection and Quality Control

To enhance defect detection, the company installed IoT-enabled smart sensors on its production lines. These sensors collected detailed data on various aspects of production, such as temperature, pressure, and vibration, which could indicate potential quality issues.

Benefits of Smart Sensors:

Real-Time Monitoring: Sensors captured data in real-time, providing continuous insights into the production environment.

Predictive Maintenance: Data from sensors helped identify equipment that was likely to fail, enabling preventive maintenance before defects occurred.

Enhanced Defect Detection: By analyzing patterns in sensor data, the company could detect deviations indicative of defects earlier in the production process.

The use of smart sensors reduced the reliance on manual inspections and minimized human error, resulting in more accurate defect detection and overall improvement in product quality.

3. AI and Machine Learning for Predictive Quality Analytics

Artificial intelligence and machine learning played a significant role in predictive quality analytics. The company utilized AI algorithms to analyze historical quality data and predict potential issues in production. This proactive approach allowed the quality team to address issues before they impacted the final product.

Applications of AI and ML:

Predictive Quality Control: The AI model identified patterns associated with common defects, enabling the team to prevent issues based on these predictions.

Root Cause Analysis: Machine learning algorithms pinpointed the root causes of quality issues, helping the company make data-driven improvements to processes.

Dynamic Adjustments: Based on AI insights, production parameters were adjusted dynamically to maintain optimal quality.

By integrating AI into their quality management processes, the company significantly reduced the incidence of defects, thereby lowering rework and scrap rates.

4. Blockchain for Supplier Quality Assurance and Transparency

Supplier quality control was another critical area addressed in the digital transformation initiative. The company implemented a blockchain-based platform to improve transparency and traceability in its supplier network. Each supplier's quality data, including inspection results, certifications, and production standards, was stored on the blockchain.

Benefits of Blockchain Implementation:

Enhanced Transparency: Blockchain allowed the company to verify supplier quality data in real-time, reducing the risk of quality issues from subpar materials.

Traceability: In case of a defect, the company could quickly trace the component back to its source, streamlining the recall process if necessary.

Supplier Accountability: Suppliers were held accountable for maintaining consistent quality, as their data was visible and auditable on the blockchain.

This level of transparency led to a closer partnership between the company and its suppliers, ensuring that quality standards were upheld throughout the supply chain.

Results and Benefits

The digital transformation initiative led to several measurable improvements in the company's quality management processes:

Reduced Defect Rates: The integration of AI, IoT, and real-time data analytics reduced defect rates by 30%. By identifying quality issues earlier in the production process, the company minimized rework and enhanced product quality.

Improved Consistency Across Facilities: The centralized QMS and standardized quality data across locations improved consistency in quality standards, leading to higher customer satisfaction.

Enhanced Supplier Quality Control: The blockchain-based supplier quality assurance system reduced the number of defects originating from suppliers by 20%, thanks to improved transparency and traceability.

Increased Operational Efficiency: Automation and predictive maintenance reduced downtime by 15%, as machines were maintained proactively, and manual inspection tasks were streamlined.

Higher Customer Satisfaction and Reduced Recalls: By delivering consistent and high-quality products, the company saw an increase in customer satisfaction scores. Additionally, the improved defect detection and traceability minimized the risk of costly recalls.

Cost Savings: Reduced defect rates and lower scrap and rework costs resulted in significant cost savings, improving the company's profitability.

Lessons Learned and Future Outlook

This case study highlights several key lessons and best practices for companies undergoing digital transformation in quality management:

Data Integration is Critical: A centralized QMS with integrated data sources is essential for consistency in quality management across multiple locations.

IoT and AI Enable Proactive Quality Control: Real-time data from IoT sensors and predictive analytics from AI allow companies to move from reactive to proactive quality management.

Blockchain Enhances Trust and Accountability in Supply Chains: By implementing blockchain, companies can improve supplier quality control and traceability, fostering a culture of transparency and accountability.

As the company continues its digital transformation journey, it aims to explore additional emerging technologies, such as advanced robotics and augmented reality, for even greater improvements in quality management. With a resilient, data-driven QMS in place, the company is well-positioned to adapt to future challenges and maintain high standards in an increasingly competitive market.

This case demonstrates the power of digital tools in enhancing quality processes, resulting in a stronger competitive advantage and greater customer trust. For organizations in the manufacturing sector, adopting similar digital solutions can drive lasting improvements in quality management and overall operational performance.

12.2 Case Study 2: Healthcare Industry

12.2 Case Study 2: Healthcare Industry – Digital Quality Transformation in a Healthcare Setting

Digital transformation is revolutionizing the healthcare industry, fundamentally altering how quality management is approached to enhance patient safety, service efficiency, and care outcomes. This case study explores how a prominent healthcare organization implemented digital quality transformation, focusing on the technological advancements that facilitated real-time monitoring, improved patient care, and streamlined compliance with healthcare standards. The study outlines the challenges faced, the digital solutions adopted, and the resulting improvements.

Background: Organization Profile and Initial Challenges

Organization Profile:

The healthcare organization highlighted here is a large, multispecialty hospital group serving millions of patients annually. With multiple locations and a range of services, the organization is recognized for its commitment to high-quality patient care and compliance with healthcare regulations.

Initial Challenges:

Before digital transformation, the organization struggled with several quality management issues typical in healthcare settings:

Fragmented Data Across Departments: Patient data and quality metrics were often stored in disparate systems across departments, leading to data silos and inconsistencies.

Manual Processes for Quality Monitoring: Quality reporting and compliance audits relied heavily on manual data entry and paperwork, resulting in delays and errors.

Limited Real-Time Insights: The organization lacked the capability for real-time monitoring of patient health data and process quality, making it difficult to address issues promptly.

Compliance Complexity: Meeting regulatory standards, such as those set by the Joint Commission and HIPAA, required significant time and resources due to the complexity of manually managing compliance protocols.

These challenges highlighted the need for a unified, digital approach to quality management that would enable better data integration, real-time insights, and seamless compliance.

Digital Quality Transformation Initiative

The hospital group's digital quality transformation focused on creating a centralized, data-driven system that leveraged technologies like Electronic Health Records (EHR), Internet of Things (IoT) devices, artificial intelligence (AI), and machine learning (ML). This approach was designed to improve data accessibility, automate quality monitoring, and enhance patient care.

1. Implementing a Centralized Electronic Health Record (EHR) System

One of the first steps was to implement a comprehensive EHR system that would serve as a unified data repository for patient records, quality metrics, and treatment histories across all departments. This EHR system integrated data from different sources, including diagnostic labs, imaging departments, and patient monitoring devices, into a single, accessible platform.

Key Features of the EHR System:

Interoperability: Integrated seamlessly with existing systems in various departments, enabling real-time data sharing and access.

Automated Data Collection: Reduced the need for manual data entry, ensuring data accuracy and availability.

Customizable Dashboards: Provided healthcare professionals with real-time insights into patient care quality metrics and flagged any deviations from care standards.

By integrating patient data, the EHR system allowed healthcare professionals to make data-informed decisions promptly, enhancing the quality and timeliness of patient care.

2. IoT-Enabled Patient Monitoring for Real-Time Quality Assurance

To improve real-time quality monitoring, the hospital installed IoT-enabled patient monitoring devices throughout critical care units and patient rooms. These devices collected continuous data on vital signs, medication administration, and equipment functionality.

Benefits of IoT in Quality Management:

Continuous Monitoring: Allowed for 24/7 monitoring of patient health metrics, alerting healthcare staff to any anomalies.

Data-Driven Alerts: Automatically triggered alerts for early intervention if vital signs indicated potential health risks, thus improving patient safety.

Equipment Quality Monitoring: Tracked medical equipment status, ensuring that devices were functioning correctly and available when needed.

This real-time monitoring helped reduce the risk of human error and enabled healthcare staff to respond to potential quality issues or patient emergencies instantly, significantly improving patient outcomes.

3. AI and ML for Predictive Quality Analytics

To further enhance quality management, the hospital integrated AI and ML into its EHR system to predict patient care needs and prevent potential quality issues. These AI-driven insights were used for both predictive patient care and quality control in treatment processes.

Applications of AI and ML:

Predictive Patient Care: Machine learning models analyzed historical data and patient health indicators to predict complications, such as infections or readmissions, enabling preventive interventions.

Quality Control in Treatment: AI algorithms monitored treatment protocols, identifying deviations or suboptimal practices in real-time, allowing for immediate corrective actions.

Operational Efficiency: AI helped optimize staff allocation and resource management, ensuring that quality of care was maintained even during high patient influx periods.

The predictive capabilities of AI and ML helped prevent adverse patient outcomes, reduce hospital readmissions, and optimize resource allocation, all of which contributed to higher quality care.

4. Digital Tools for Compliance and Risk Management

Healthcare organizations are subject to stringent regulatory standards and risk management requirements. The hospital implemented digital tools specifically designed to automate compliance monitoring, document management, and risk assessment.

Benefits of Digital Compliance Tools:

Automated Compliance Tracking: The digital compliance tools tracked regulatory standards, including HIPAA and Joint Commission requirements, reducing the administrative burden.

Real-Time Risk Assessment: Identified potential areas of non-compliance in real-time, allowing the quality management team to take preventive measures.

Streamlined Documentation: Enabled electronic document management, ensuring that compliance documentation was accurate, updated, and easily accessible.

By automating compliance processes, the hospital minimized risks related to regulatory fines and penalties, reducing the time required for compliance reporting and audits.

Results and Benefits

The digital quality transformation led to several impactful results for the hospital group:

Improved Patient Safety: IoT-enabled patient monitoring and predictive AI analytics reduced the likelihood of adverse events, enhancing patient safety across departments.

Enhanced Data Accessibility and Integration: The centralized EHR system provided a single source of truth for patient data, reducing data silos and ensuring that healthcare professionals had the information they needed at their fingertips.

Reduced Error Rates: By automating data entry and quality monitoring, the hospital experienced fewer errors, particularly in areas related to medication administration and patient documentation.

Faster Response Times: Real-time monitoring and data-driven alerts enabled healthcare staff to respond to patient needs more rapidly, improving patient outcomes and reducing emergency intervention rates.

Efficient Compliance Management: Automated compliance tracking streamlined regulatory processes, saving significant time and reducing the risk of non-compliance.

Cost Savings and Resource Optimization: The predictive capabilities of AI and ML allowed for better resource allocation, ensuring that staffing and equipment were optimized to meet patient demand without compromising quality.

Lessons Learned and Future Outlook

This case study provides valuable insights into best practices and considerations for healthcare organizations undertaking digital transformation:

Data Centralization is Essential: A unified EHR system can provide a foundation for consistent quality management, integrating data across departments and reducing information silos.

Real-Time Monitoring Enhances Patient Outcomes: IoT devices and automated monitoring enable rapid response to patient needs, improving safety and care quality.

AI and Predictive Analytics Transform Patient Care: AI-driven insights allow healthcare providers to proactively manage patient needs, preventing complications and optimizing resource use.

Looking ahead, the hospital plans to expand its digital capabilities, exploring technologies like robotic process automation (RPA) for administrative tasks and augmented reality (AR) for surgical training and remote consultations. With a strong digital foundation, the organization is well-prepared to meet future challenges, continue enhancing care quality, and remain at the forefront of healthcare innovation.

This case illustrates the profound impact of digital tools in transforming quality management within healthcare, benefiting both the organization and its patients. For healthcare providers, adopting a similar digital approach can lead to safer, more efficient, and higher-quality care.

12.3 Case Study 3: Technology Sector

12.3 Case Study 3: Technology Sector – Quality Management Advancements in a Tech Company

In the fast-evolving technology sector, quality management (QM) has taken on a new level of importance as companies strive to develop products that meet high standards in functionality, reliability, and user experience. This case study examines a global technology company that implemented advanced quality management practices through digital transformation to enhance product quality, speed up innovation, and improve customer satisfaction. By leveraging agile methods, artificial intelligence (AI), and continuous feedback loops, the company achieved substantial gains in quality while accelerating product delivery.

Background: Organization Profile and Initial Challenges

Organization Profile:

The company featured in this case study is a leading tech giant known for its innovation in consumer electronics, software development, and digital services. With products used by millions worldwide, the company is committed to delivering superior quality and user satisfaction, positioning quality management as a strategic priority.

Initial Challenges:

As the company scaled its product portfolio, several quality management challenges emerged, such as:

Complex Product Ecosystem: Managing quality across a wide range of interconnected hardware and software products made it difficult to ensure consistent standards.

Rapid Release Cycles: To stay competitive, the company had to deliver frequent product updates and new features, making it hard to thoroughly test and ensure quality.

High Customer Expectations: Users of the company's products demanded flawless performance, quick resolutions for issues, and continuous improvement.

Data Overload: The company collected vast amounts of data from multiple sources, but this data was not always accessible in real-time for actionable insights.

Given these challenges, the company sought to overhaul its quality management processes by integrating advanced technologies and adopting agile quality practices.

Digital Quality Transformation Initiative

To address its quality management challenges, the tech company embarked on a digital transformation initiative, with a focus on agile methodologies, AI, machine learning (ML), and data-driven quality control. This strategy aimed to establish a more responsive, customer-focused approach to quality management.

1. Implementing Agile Quality Management

The company adopted an agile quality management framework to replace its traditional, linear approach to product development and quality control. By transitioning to agile, the company could rapidly iterate on product improvements, respond quickly to customer feedback, and adapt to changing market demands.

Key Components of Agile Quality Management:

Cross-Functional Teams: Quality engineers, product developers, and customer support teams collaborated in small, cross-functional teams to ensure quality was integrated into every stage of development.

Iterative Testing and Development: Shorter, iterative cycles allowed the company to continuously test products, identify issues, and implement fixes, ensuring that quality was an ongoing process.

Continuous Integration (CI) and Continuous Delivery (CD): Automated CI/CD pipelines facilitated rapid code deployment and testing, enabling the company to release new features with minimal delays and maximum quality.

This agile approach empowered the company to improve quality throughout the product lifecycle, adapting quickly to issues without sacrificing development speed.

2. AI and ML for Predictive Quality Management

To proactively address quality issues, the company invested in AI and ML tools that provided predictive insights into potential quality risks and customer concerns. By analyzing historical data and current product performance, these technologies allowed the company to identify patterns and make data-informed decisions to improve quality.

Applications of AI and ML:

Predictive Maintenance for Hardware Products: For its hardware products, AI models analyzed usage data to predict failures before they occurred, prompting preventive maintenance or firmware updates that minimized downtime for customers.

Anomaly Detection in Software Code: ML algorithms detected anomalies and vulnerabilities in software code during the development process, reducing the likelihood of bugs and improving product security.

Customer Sentiment Analysis: Using AI-driven sentiment analysis, the company monitored customer feedback from social media and support tickets, identifying emerging quality issues and prioritizing them based on user impact.

These predictive insights allowed the company to address potential quality issues early, resulting in fewer bugs, better product performance, and a more satisfying user experience.

3. Integrating Real-Time Quality Monitoring

To ensure quality across the product ecosystem, the company implemented real-time monitoring tools that collected and analyzed data from various sources, such as production lines, customer usage, and device diagnostics. Real-time monitoring was essential in quickly detecting and addressing quality issues as they arose.

Real-Time Monitoring Features:

Dashboard Analytics for Product Performance: Customizable dashboards provided stakeholders with a clear view of quality metrics in real time, helping them identify and address issues across products.

Automated Alerts for Quality Issues: If specific metrics fell outside acceptable ranges, the system triggered alerts for quality control teams to investigate and resolve the issue immediately.

Remote Diagnostics for Hardware Products: The company enabled remote diagnostic capabilities, allowing quality teams to troubleshoot issues with products already in customers' hands, reducing the need for recalls or replacements.

Real-time monitoring facilitated a proactive approach to quality management, ensuring that the company could swiftly address potential issues and minimize their impact on customers.

4. Leveraging Customer Feedback and Continuous Improvement Loops

Customer satisfaction was a critical measure of quality for the company, which used digital tools to capture and act on customer feedback in real time. These feedback loops allowed the company to make data-driven adjustments that aligned with user expectations and enhanced product quality.

Digital Feedback Mechanisms:

In-App Feedback Channels: Customers were encouraged to provide feedback directly within apps and software, allowing the company to gather insights about functionality, usability, and potential issues.

Social Media and Support Analysis: The company monitored social media and support tickets using AI-driven sentiment analysis tools to track emerging quality concerns.

Rapid Response to User Feedback: With agile methodologies in place, the company quickly incorporated user feedback into development cycles, improving product features, addressing bugs, and refining the user experience.

This customer-centric approach to quality fostered a culture of continuous improvement, where feedback was used as a valuable input for product and quality management strategies.

Results and Benefits

The digital quality transformation led to significant improvements across various quality metrics, including:

Increased Product Reliability: Predictive AI and ML tools helped the company proactively identify and address potential product issues, improving product reliability and reducing customer complaints.

Enhanced Customer Satisfaction: Real-time feedback loops and agile responsiveness resulted in faster issue resolution and better product performance, leading to higher customer satisfaction scores.

Faster Time-to-Market: Agile methods and automated CI/CD pipelines reduced the time required to release updates and new features, allowing the company to stay competitive in a rapidly evolving market.

Data-Driven Quality Insights: The company's use of real-time monitoring and data analytics provided actionable insights, allowing teams to make quality improvements based on actual usage data.

Improved Compliance and Security: Automated anomaly detection and rigorous testing protocols reduced security vulnerabilities and helped the company comply with industry standards and regulations.

These advancements underscored the value of integrating digital tools and agile practices in quality management, resulting in more resilient products, a competitive edge, and a loyal customer base.

Lessons Learned and Future Outlook

This case study offers several key lessons for companies seeking to enhance quality management in the technology sector:

Agile and Cross-Functional Collaboration is Key: Integrating quality management into agile workflows and fostering cross-functional collaboration can accelerate quality improvements and align them with customer needs.

Predictive Tools Enhance Proactivity: AI and ML models provide invaluable predictive insights, allowing companies to address quality issues before they affect customers, thus improving reliability and reducing costs.

Real-Time Monitoring Adds Value: Continuous quality monitoring across the product ecosystem enables early detection of issues, reducing their impact and enabling a proactive quality approach.

As the company continues its digital transformation, it plans to explore emerging technologies, such as augmented reality (AR) for remote troubleshooting and blockchain for quality assurance in its supply chain. With a solid foundation in digital quality management, the company is well-equipped to navigate future challenges, ensure product excellence, and maintain its leadership in the tech industry.

This case illustrates how tech companies can leverage digital tools to transform quality management, foster a customer-centric approach, and deliver high-quality, innovative products in a competitive market.

13. The Future of Quality Management in the Digital Age

The digital age has revolutionized quality management, paving the way for more efficient, accurate, and responsive systems that can adapt to rapid technological advancements and changing consumer expectations. Quality management (QM) has moved beyond traditional processes to encompass innovative technologies that drive continuous improvement, predictive maintenance, and personalized customer experiences. This chapter explores the emerging trends and innovations that are reshaping the future of quality management, with a focus on artificial intelligence (AI), automation, digital twins, and augmented reality (AR).

13.1 Emerging Trends and Innovations

Artificial Intelligence (AI) in Quality Management

AI is a key enabler of digital transformation in quality management. By leveraging machine learning (ML) and other AI-driven tools, organizations can process massive datasets, extract actionable insights, and make data-driven decisions. AI enhances quality management by predicting potential defects, identifying patterns in production, and improving accuracy in quality checks.

Applications of AI in Quality Management:

Predictive Analytics for Defect Prevention: AI-powered predictive analytics models analyze data from past production cycles to forecast quality issues before they occur. By identifying potential risks early, manufacturers can implement corrective measures, leading to fewer defects and a reduction in rework costs.

AI-Based Inspection Systems: Machine learning models are used to improve inspection accuracy, especially in visual quality control processes. AI-driven image recognition software can identify minute defects that may be missed by human inspectors, improving quality assurance in production lines.

Automated Root Cause Analysis: AI helps in identifying the root cause of quality issues by analyzing patterns in data. Through natural language processing (NLP) and ML algorithms, quality management systems can interpret data from production logs, maintenance reports, and even customer feedback to pinpoint problem sources efficiently.

The future of AI in quality management includes real-time anomaly detection, where quality issues are identified and resolved instantly, further minimizing downtime and improving customer satisfaction.

Automation in Quality Management

Automation in quality management streamlines routine tasks, reduces human error, and improves efficiency across production processes. Robotics and process automation are transforming quality control by automating repetitive inspections, measurements, and data collection.

Key Areas of Automation in Quality Management:

Automated Data Collection and Analysis: Automation tools collect data from various sources, such as production machines and IoT sensors, in real time. This data is then automatically analyzed to check for discrepancies, enabling faster identification of quality issues.

Robotic Process Automation (RPA) for Quality Checks: RPA is used to automate quality checks, especially in high-volume production environments. Robots can perform consistent inspections, measurements, and adjustments, ensuring that each product meets quality standards without the need for manual oversight.

Automated Reporting and Documentation: Quality management systems generate reports and documentation automatically, reducing paperwork and ensuring compliance with regulatory standards. Automated documentation also makes it easier to track quality trends over time.

Automation enables continuous quality control, enhancing production efficiency and helping organizations meet high standards with minimal manual intervention. This is especially valuable in industries with strict regulatory requirements, such as pharmaceuticals and aerospace.

Digital Twins in Quality Management

Digital twins—virtual representations of physical assets—are transforming how organizations manage and improve product quality. By creating a digital twin of a product, process, or system, companies can simulate, monitor, and optimize performance in real-time.

Applications of Digital Twins in Quality Management:

Simulating Production Scenarios: Digital twins allow companies to simulate different production scenarios, identifying potential quality issues before actual production. This simulation can help in adjusting parameters, such as material specifications or environmental factors, to ensure optimal quality.

Real-Time Monitoring and Predictive Maintenance: Digital twins enable real-time monitoring of equipment and systems, helping in predicting and preventing breakdowns. By comparing live data with the digital twin model, quality managers can detect deviations and address them proactively.

Product Lifecycle Management: A digital twin accompanies a product throughout its lifecycle, from design to disposal. By analyzing performance data over time, organizations can identify patterns that affect quality and make improvements to future product designs.

Digital twins offer an innovative approach to quality management, combining real-time data with simulation capabilities to provide a comprehensive view of quality across the production lifecycle.

Augmented Reality (AR) in Quality Management

Augmented reality (AR) is emerging as a valuable tool in quality management, offering immersive experiences that enhance training, inspections, and maintenance activities. AR overlays digital information on the physical world, helping workers visualize quality standards, identify defects, and perform tasks more accurately.

AR Applications in Quality Management:

Enhanced Quality Inspections: AR devices, such as smart glasses, allow workers to see real-time data, such as product specifications and quality checklists, directly on their viewfinder. This hands-free access to information ensures that each step in the inspection process is followed precisely.

Training and Skill Development: AR-based training modules can simulate quality control tasks, allowing workers to practice in a virtual environment before handling actual products. This immersive training method improves retention and reduces errors in real-world inspections.

Remote Assistance for Quality Issues: Through AR, experts can remotely guide on-site workers in real time. Quality managers can see exactly what the worker sees and provide guidance on resolving issues, making troubleshooting more efficient and minimizing downtime.

AR adds a layer of interactivity and precision to quality management, empowering workers to perform quality checks with higher accuracy and confidence.

The Future Outlook for Quality Management in the Digital Age

The integration of AI, automation, digital twins, and AR in quality management signifies a shift towards data-driven, predictive, and adaptive quality systems. These technologies will continue to evolve, further enhancing quality management capabilities across industries.

Future Trends:

Interconnected Quality Systems: Quality management systems (QMS) will increasingly integrate with enterprise systems, such as ERP and supply chain platforms, to create an interconnected quality network. This integration enables seamless data flow and holistic quality insights across the organization.

Increased Personalization in Quality Standards: As customer expectations become more individualized, companies will develop quality standards that cater to personalized demands. By leveraging data analytics and AI, companies can customize quality metrics to align with specific customer needs.

Sustainability and Quality Integration: Future quality management will prioritize sustainability, assessing products and processes based on their environmental impact. Quality criteria will expand to include sustainability metrics, such as waste reduction, recyclability, and energy efficiency.

Enhanced Cybersecurity in Quality Systems: As quality management becomes more digital, cybersecurity will become a priority. Protecting quality data and ensuring the security of digital tools will be essential to prevent disruptions and maintain customer trust.

The digital transformation of quality management is still in its early stages, and these emerging technologies will continue to shape the industry, creating opportunities for more responsive, accurate, and customer-focused quality systems. Organizations that embrace these innovations will not only improve product quality but also achieve a competitive advantage in the digital age.

13.2 Preparing for the Future of Digital Quality Management

As digital transformation accelerates, the future of quality management will demand a blend of new skills, adaptive strategies, and a forward-thinking approach to leverage the potential of emerging technologies. Organizations must foster a culture of continuous learning, equip teams with the necessary tools, and implement strategies that promote agility, resilience, and innovation in their quality management practices. This section explores the essential skills, strategies, and adaptability measures that organizations can adopt to future-proof their quality management processes.

Skills Needed for the Future of Digital Quality Management

The digital evolution in quality management emphasizes data literacy, technical proficiency, and critical thinking. As traditional quality roles evolve, teams will need to develop both hard and soft skills that align with the demands of modern quality management.

1. Data Literacy and Analytical Skills

The ability to interpret and analyze data accurately will be central to quality management. As companies gather vast amounts of data from IoT sensors, customer feedback, and other digital sources, quality teams must be skilled in:

Data Collection and Cleansing: Knowing how to gather, organize, and clean data for accuracy.

Statistical Analysis: Using statistical tools to identify patterns, trends, and root causes of quality issues.

Predictive Analytics: Applying machine learning and predictive models to foresee potential issues and address them proactively.

Training employees in data science and analytical software will enable quality managers to make data-informed decisions, increase accuracy, and optimize processes.

2. Technical Proficiency with Digital Tools and Systems

With quality management becoming increasingly technology-driven, familiarity with digital tools is crucial. Key skills in this area include:

Using Quality Management Systems (QMS): Proficiency in software like SAP, Oracle Quality Management, and specialized QMS platforms.

Automation Tools and Robotics: Understanding the fundamentals of automation, such as robotic process automation (RPA) for automating routine quality checks.

IoT and Sensor Technology: Knowing how to work with IoT devices and interpret sensor data for real-time monitoring.

Technical skills should be complemented with ongoing training to keep pace with advancements and ensure seamless integration of technology into quality processes.

3. Artificial Intelligence (AI) and Machine Learning (ML) Familiarity

AI and ML are powerful tools for predictive maintenance, defect detection, and root cause analysis. Quality professionals will benefit from:

Basic AI/ML Concepts: Understanding core concepts like supervised and unsupervised learning.

AI Tools and Software: Familiarity with platforms like Python, R, or TensorFlow to interpret AI-driven quality insights.

Practical Applications: Knowing how AI/ML models can improve quality processes and lead to proactive quality control.

Training in AI and ML applications will empower quality teams to identify and mitigate issues more effectively, improving accuracy and reducing costs.

4. Change Management and Adaptability

As organizations adopt new technologies, the ability to manage change will be essential. Skills in change management will help teams:

Communicate Benefits: Clearly convey how digital transformation improves quality processes to stakeholders.

Manage Resistance to Change: Address employee concerns and create a positive transition.

Continuous Improvement Mindset: Embrace change as an opportunity to refine processes and explore innovative solutions.

Change management training should be included in leadership development programs to prepare managers to guide teams through transformations smoothly.

5. Soft Skills: Collaboration and Communication

Digital quality management requires collaboration across departments such as IT, production, and customer service. Strong soft skills will help quality professionals:

Work with Cross-Functional Teams: Coordinate efforts with different departments to implement quality solutions.

Communicate Insights: Clearly present data-driven insights to decision-makers.

Foster a Data-Driven Culture: Encourage a culture of data-driven thinking throughout the organization.

Soft skills training, including effective communication and collaboration techniques, will be crucial as organizations strive to integrate digital quality processes company-wide.

Strategies for Future-Ready Quality Management

Adopting a proactive, strategic approach is essential for successful digital quality management. Here are key strategies to prepare for the future:

1. Investing in Scalable Technology Infrastructure

Organizations should prioritize investments in scalable, flexible infrastructure to support evolving quality management needs. A strong foundation enables integration of new tools without major disruptions.

Cloud-Based Quality Management Systems: Cloud platforms offer flexibility, allowing organizations to scale up or down based on needs.

Modular Architecture: A modular approach enables seamless integration of new technologies, such as AI tools or blockchain, as they become relevant.

Data Storage and Security: Investing in secure, high-capacity storage solutions ensures that quality data remains accessible, reliable, and protected.

Scalable infrastructure allows companies to remain adaptable, efficiently incorporating new technologies to improve quality management.

2. Developing a Data-Driven Quality Management Framework

A data-driven framework provides a structured approach to utilizing data for continuous improvement.

Standardized Data Collection Processes: Establish consistent methods for collecting quality data across different departments.

Data Analysis Protocols: Create protocols for analyzing data, enabling faster identification of trends and root causes of issues.

Data Governance: Ensure data accuracy, security, and compliance with regulations through a dedicated data governance strategy.

By aligning data collection and analysis with organizational goals, companies can leverage insights to drive quality improvements effectively.

3. Implementing Agile Quality Management Principles

Adopting agile principles in quality management enhances flexibility and responsiveness.

Iterative Process Improvements: Embrace a cycle of continuous assessment and improvement, allowing teams to refine quality processes as needs evolve.

Cross-Functional Collaboration: Agile encourages close collaboration among departments, enabling rapid adjustments to quality processes.

Customer Feedback Loops: Use customer insights to adapt and improve quality measures in real-time.

Agile quality management helps companies stay adaptable in a fast-paced environment, making quality systems more responsive to customer needs and industry changes.

4. Fostering a Culture of Continuous Improvement and Innovation

A culture that values continuous improvement and innovation is essential for long-term success.

Encourage Experimentation: Promote a mindset where employees are encouraged to experiment with new ideas and approaches to quality.

Reward Quality Improvement Initiatives: Recognize and reward efforts to enhance quality, reinforcing a culture of excellence.

Leadership Support: Strong leadership support for quality initiatives fosters employee commitment to continuous improvement.

A culture of innovation encourages employees to think proactively and contribute to the evolution of quality practices, driving organizational success.

Building Adaptability for the Future

Adaptability will be crucial in maintaining high-quality standards in an era of rapid technological change. Here's how organizations can cultivate adaptability:

1. Continuous Learning and Development Programs

Continuous learning is essential for staying current with new technologies and methodologies.

Regular Training on Emerging Technologies: Provide ongoing training in AI, IoT, blockchain, and other relevant technologies.

Certifications and Professional Development: Encourage employees to pursue certifications in quality management, data analysis, and technology-specific courses.

Cross-Training Programs: Offer cross-training to broaden employees' skill sets, making them versatile and adaptable.

Continuous learning keeps teams prepared to leverage new tools and processes, ensuring that quality management remains at the forefront of innovation.

2. Flexible Quality Processes

Flexibility in quality processes enables rapid adaptation to changes in technology, customer expectations, and industry standards.

Modular Process Design: Design quality processes that can be adapted or replaced without disrupting other systems.

Real-Time Quality Monitoring: Use IoT and digital twins for real-time monitoring, allowing teams to respond quickly to quality issues.

Feedback-Driven Adjustments: Regularly gather feedback from employees, customers, and stakeholders to refine quality processes.

Flexibility in quality processes allows organizations to maintain high standards while accommodating changes in the business environment.

3. Proactive Risk Management

Digital quality management involves unique risks, such as data privacy issues and cybersecurity threats.

Identify Emerging Risks: Regularly assess and update risk management strategies to account for new digital risks.

Cybersecurity Training: Educate teams on cybersecurity best practices to safeguard quality data and maintain system integrity.

Compliance with Digital Standards: Adhere to digital quality standards, such as ISO 27001, to ensure data protection and minimize risks.

Proactive risk management builds resilience in quality systems, ensuring that companies can withstand challenges associated with digital transformation.

The future of digital quality management requires a holistic approach that combines technical skills, adaptable strategies, and a culture of continuous improvement. By investing in data literacy, technical proficiency, and agile quality processes, organizations can prepare for upcoming changes in quality management. Moreover, fostering a continuous learning culture and developing flexible, resilient systems will allow companies to harness the power of emerging technologies, such as AI, automation, digital twins, and AR, to achieve long-term success in quality management.

13.3 Concluding Thoughts on Quality Management in the Digital Age

The digital age has ushered in transformative changes for quality management, reshaping how organizations perceive, monitor, and ensure quality across all stages of production and service delivery. In this new era, quality management has evolved from a system of reactive inspections to a proactive, data-driven approach that integrates advanced technology and emphasizes continuous improvement. Embracing digital transformation in quality management is no longer optional; it is essential for organizations to stay competitive, adapt to rapidly changing customer expectations, and navigate the complexities of a global marketplace.

This section offers a final reflection on the journey of quality management transformation, highlighting the core themes and providing insights into what the future may hold for organizations committed to digital quality excellence.

Embracing Technology for Quality Excellence

Digital transformation in quality management has been made possible by the proliferation of technology, including AI, IoT, blockchain, data analytics, and automation. These advancements enable organizations to perform real-time monitoring, predictive maintenance, and precision-driven process improvements. Each of these technologies plays a unique role:

AI and Machine Learning empower organizations to predict quality issues before they occur, drive root cause analysis, and enhance decision-making processes.

IoT Sensors and Data Analytics provide real-time visibility into manufacturing and supply chain processes, allowing for timely quality checks and data-driven insights.

Blockchain brings transparency and traceability, especially in supply chain quality assurance, establishing trust and accountability.

Automation and Robotics streamline repetitive tasks, reduce human error, and maintain consistent quality levels.

The adoption of these technologies represents a fundamental shift from traditional methods, making quality management a proactive and efficient system that anticipates issues rather than merely reacting to them. For organizations that are open to innovation and adaptability, these technologies provide a pathway to achieve higher standards of quality at greater speeds and lower costs.

Building a Culture of Continuous Improvement and Innovation

While technology forms the backbone of digital quality management, a forward-thinking organizational culture is equally vital. For digital transformation to thrive, companies must foster a culture of continuous improvement and innovation. This culture is characterized by:

Employee Empowerment: Encouraging all team members to contribute ideas and solutions for quality improvements helps foster a sense of ownership and accountability.

Open Communication: Transparent and open communication across departments promotes collaboration, helping to integrate quality into every phase of the production and service cycle.

Customer-Centricity: Keeping the customer at the center of quality decisions ensures that digital quality initiatives align with customer needs and expectations.

Learning and Development: As digital tools and methods continue to evolve, organizations must invest in ongoing training and professional development to build digital competencies across teams.

Developing this culture requires time, commitment, and buy-in from leadership. It is an investment that pays off through a resilient and innovative approach to quality that can withstand the disruptions and demands of the digital age.

Navigating Challenges in Digital Quality Transformation

The path to digital quality transformation is not without its challenges. Organizations often face obstacles such as data security risks, high implementation costs, and the need for change management. Data security and privacy have become central concerns as organizations collect vast amounts of data for quality analytics. Cybersecurity strategies, compliant with digital standards such as ISO 27001, are essential to protect sensitive information and maintain trust.

The financial investment in digital quality management systems, automation tools, and data infrastructure is significant, but organizations must view these costs as investments in long-term quality resilience and competitiveness. Additionally, as processes and technologies evolve, so must the willingness of employees and managers to adapt. Successful digital quality management requires thoughtful change management strategies, fostering an environment that encourages embracing new methodologies rather than resisting them.

Future-Proofing Quality with Agility and Adaptability

In an age of rapid technological change, agility and adaptability are essential qualities for any organization aiming to sustain quality excellence. Agile quality management allows organizations to respond quickly to shifts in market conditions, customer expectations, and technological advancements. For instance, using iterative improvements and cross-functional collaboration, organizations can continually refine quality standards and processes to better align with real-time data insights.

Adopting agile practices also encourages flexibility, which is crucial as new technologies like digital twins, AI, and augmented reality continue to emerge. Digital quality management strategies must be flexible enough to integrate these advancements as they become relevant. Organizations that cultivate an adaptable approach to quality management will not only respond more effectively to new challenges but also capture opportunities for innovation and growth.

277

Final Insights on the Digital Quality Transformation Journey

The journey to digital quality management is a continuous one, with no definitive endpoint. As technologies evolve and customer expectations grow, quality management will also need to adapt, becoming more integrated, data-driven, and customer-focused. The transformation to digital quality management is not merely about implementing technology but about reshaping the organization's philosophy, strategy, and culture around quality.

Organizations that successfully transform their quality management practices in the digital age will reap numerous benefits, including enhanced customer satisfaction, operational efficiency, and brand reputation. They will be better equipped to meet regulatory requirements, stay competitive, and innovate in response to market demands. By embracing a holistic approach that includes advanced technology, a culture of improvement, risk management, and a commitment to agility, these organizations position themselves to lead in an era where quality is paramount to business success.

In conclusion, the digital transformation of quality management represents a powerful shift toward smarter, faster, and more resilient quality systems. Organizations that proactively adopt digital tools and cultivate a mindset of continuous improvement will be well-prepared to meet the demands of the digital age and beyond, turning quality management into a strategic advantage in an increasingly complex world.

Appendices and Resources

Glossary of Terms

A

Agile Quality Management: A flexible approach to quality management that emphasizes iterative processes, collaboration, and customer feedback.

B

Blockchain: A decentralized digital ledger that records transactions across many computers securely, ensuring transparency and traceability.

C

Customer Satisfaction Score (CSAT): A measurement used to gauge customer satisfaction with a product or service, typically expressed as a percentage.

D

Data Analytics: The process of examining data sets to draw conclusions about the information they contain, often using statistical tools and software.

E

Evidence-Based Decision Making: The practice of making decisions based on the analysis of data and factual evidence rather than intuition or observation alone.

I

Internet of Things (IoT): A network of interconnected devices that communicate and exchange data over the internet, often used for real-time monitoring.

M

Machine Learning (ML): A subset of artificial intelligence that enables systems to learn from data, identify patterns, and make decisions with minimal human intervention.

P

Predictive Analytics: Techniques that use statistical algorithms and machine learning to identify the likelihood of future outcomes based on historical data.

Q

Quality Management System (QMS): A structured system that documents processes, procedures, and responsibilities for achieving quality policies and objectives.

S

Statistical Process Control (SPC): A method of quality control that uses statistical methods to monitor and control a process, ensuring that it operates at its full potential.

T

Total Quality Management (TQM): A management approach aimed at long-term success through customer satisfaction, involving all members of an organization in improving processes, products, services, and the culture.

Key Quality Standards and Frameworks

ISO 9001

Overview: An international standard that specifies requirements for a quality management system (QMS). It is designed to help organizations ensure they meet customer and other stakeholder needs within statutory and regulatory requirements.

Key Elements: Customer focus, leadership, engagement of people, process approach, improvement, evidence-based decision making, and relationship management.

ISO 27001

Overview: A specification for an information security management system (ISMS). It provides a framework for managing sensitive company information, ensuring data security and privacy.

Key Elements: Risk assessment and management, security controls, ongoing monitoring, and compliance with legal requirements.

Six Sigma

Overview: A set of techniques and tools for process improvement, aimed at reducing defects and variability in processes. Six Sigma uses a data-driven approach and statistical methods.

Key Elements: Define, Measure, Analyze, Improve, Control (DMAIC) methodology, and a focus on quality improvement at every organizational level.

Lean

Overview: A management philosophy that focuses on minimizing waste within manufacturing systems while simultaneously maximizing productivity. It emphasizes value creation for the end customer.

Key Elements: Continuous improvement (Kaizen), value stream mapping, just-in-time production, and the 5S methodology (Sort, Set in order, Shine, Standardize, Sustain).

Baldrige Performance Excellence Framework

Overview: A framework that provides a comprehensive approach to organizational performance management. It helps organizations assess their improvement efforts and provides criteria for performance excellence.

Key Elements: Leadership, strategy, customers, measurement, analysis, knowledge management, workforce, operations, and results.

Additional Reading and Resources

Books

"The Lean Six Sigma Pocket Toolbook" by Michael L. George, et al.: A concise reference that combines Lean and Six Sigma tools and techniques.

"The Goal: A Process of Ongoing Improvement" by Eliyahu M. Goldratt: A novel that presents the Theory of Constraints and its application to manufacturing and production management.

"Quality Management Demystified" by Sid Kemp: An accessible introduction to quality management principles and practices.

Articles

"Quality Management: Principles and Practices" (Journal of Quality in Maintenance Engineering): Discusses the foundational principles of quality management and their applications.

"How Big Data is Transforming Quality Management" (Quality Digest): Explores the impact of big data on quality management practices and decision-making.

Online Resources

American Society for Quality (ASQ): asq.org - A global community of quality professionals providing resources, training, and certifications in quality management.

International Organization for Standardization (ISO): iso.org - The leading source for international standards, including quality management standards.

Webinars and Workshops

Quality Management Webinars: Various organizations offer free or low-cost webinars on topics related to quality management, digital transformation, and continuous improvement.

Workshops on Lean and Six Sigma: Many institutions provide hands-on training sessions to develop skills in Lean and Six Sigma methodologies.

Certifications

Certified Quality Manager (CQM): Offered by ASQ, this certification demonstrates the ability to manage quality in organizations effectively.

Lean Six Sigma Certification: Various levels (Yellow Belt, Green Belt, Black Belt) available through many organizations, focusing on Lean Six Sigma principles and practices.

By leveraging these resources and incorporating the principles and practices of quality management, organizations can enhance their quality processes, meet customer expectations, and drive continuous improvement in the digital age.

www.ingramcontent.com/pod-product-compliance
Lightning Source LLC
Chambersburg PA
CBHW071447220526
45472CB00003B/699